Return to K̲r̲i̲s̲t̲i̲n̲a̲ X

D0959278

Retention Wars:
The New Rules of Engagement

■ ■ ■ ■

by *Mark Levin,* CAE, CSP

B.A.I., Inc.
10015 Old Columbia Road
Suite B215
Columbia, MD 21046
Phone: 301-596-2584   Fax: 301-596-2594

To my brothers Robert and Leonard

with all my love and thanks
for making me proud every day

Retention Wars:
The New Rules of Engagement

It's Not Over 'Til It's Over

People think that Yogi Berra, the colorful Hall of Fame catcher for the New York Yankees, was just "being Yogi" when he made that famous comment years ago. Of course, Berra was talking specifically about a baseball game, trying to convey his well-known competitive spirit, and reminding everyone that he and his teammates were going to fight to the very end, no matter how far behind they might be.

Why is this message in a book about membership retention?

Simple.

It's here because it's a creed that needs to be adhered to by anyone facing the challenges of member retention in today's marketplace. The battle to get the attention, commitment, and involvement of members has never been greater. The competition for their time, money, energy, and interest has never been more formidable. The shifting needs of multiple generations, the world of the 24-hour workday, and the rush of ever-faster technologies put a greater strain on membership organizations than they have ever before had to endure.

Still, giving up is not an option. Organizations can't be content to "keep as many members as possible," and write off the others as members who weren't going to stay anyway. Giving up is not an option, because membership still matters.

Despite what some organizational leaders think, membership still matters.

A short time before this book was written, there was an article that would make anyone involved with membership retention or member service responsibilities really sit up and take notice. The article was entitled "Is Membership Dead?" It was one association management professional's view of what was happening to membership organizations in the "new" environment of the 21st century. The article was in *Executive Update*, the magazine of the Greater Washington Society of Association Executives. The article quotes the Executive Director of a major national professional organization, and the Past Chairman of the American Society of Association Executives, as believing that in many cases it costs more to attract, service, and retain a member than the member pays in dues, and how can an organization survive if each new customer costs money? He went on to say that "frankly, membership is just not that important. It carries the same weight as, say, conference attendance or book sales…" Then the article quotes several other "membership experts" who agreed in principle with this theory.

Has it come to this? Members are now a commodity, like publications and insurance?

Certainly things have changed in the membership world in the past few years, but it is difficult to envision a time when members are not important. It seems obvious that these *membership organizations* were formed to represent and serve their members. Until certain members of the association management profession convinced themselves (and others) that they were business executives, and making money was a legitimate "goal" of associations, most people in the membership development world thought so, too.

Should associations and other membership-based organizations be run in a businesslike manner? Of course they should. In many ways, these organizations are businesses. But they are unique businesses.

And what makes them unique?

The members.

Whether they are called members or customers (as some organizations prefer to call them), that doesn't change what they are. It may sound old-fashioned, but the thing that gives membership organizations their energy, their resources, and their very reason to exist is the members. That's what makes membership organizations different from the local Wal Mart. Membership organizations are the only businesses that make their "customers" pay for their services (through dues) and then ask the customers to help manage the business. No one has ever seen a manager in a Wal

Mart walking down the aisles asking customers for their input on the new Wal Mart marketing plan.

The executive who wrote the article certainly values his members. His members are hardworking, successful, and thoroughly professional. His article was meant to be a thought-provoking piece on the new challenges organizations face trying to attract and keep members, and in the article there are several examples of how associations are dealing with these challenges. Yet even the suggestion that membership is "just not that important" is cause for concern, because although the challenges and costs to get and keep members continue to grow, there really is no alternative to digging in and doing the hard work necessary to keep members.

Another thought: when the article says membership is "no more important than conference attendance and book sales," it brings up a couple of logical questions. Just who is it that will attend those conferences? Exactly who will purchase those books and other publications?

The majority of these customers will be the organization's members. That's probably the case in most membership organizations, too.

When organizational leaders claim that their organization isn't *dependent* on membership, because only a small percentage of their income (i.e. 30% or less) is derived from membership dues, that doesn't reflect the whole situation. After determining what percent of an organization's funding comes from membership dues, the organization needs to take a close look at those nondues income sources. This means the insurance plans, the meetings and conferences, the educational programs, the publication sales, etc.

If organizations go back and track the sources of their nondues income, they will, in almost all cases, find that the majority of their total income came from one common source – their members. It's the members who come to meetings and conferences, it's the members who purchase the publications, it's the members who attend the educational programs, and it's the members who sign up for distance learning sessions.

If membership organizations track their income flow, they will assuredly come to one basic conclusion:

The organizations may not be dependent on membership *dues*, but they are dependent on membership.

That's why, even in this environment, membership retention has become a true battleground for many organizations. This book is designed to give organizations the tools needed to fight that retention battle, and come out of it a winner.

In getting started in your Retention Wars, remember that it's one thing to "put some real emphasis on membership retention," and something very different to set out a retention plan that has a real chance of working. The organizations that will reap the rewards of their retention efforts are those organizations that not only have a retention plan but are *committed* to carrying it out.

The intent of this book is to clarify the challenges membership organizations face in improving their retention rates in a world that is changing faster than ever before. The book explores the phenomenon of generational diversity, and how that impacts the ability of organizations to seamlessly meld new members into their group. It will look at some traditional retention techniques and determine which can be adapted to today's retention world and which have probably outlived their usefulness. It takes an updated look at how technology can (and should) be integrated into retention activities. It tries to show how the whole concept of member involvement has changed for many members. Finally, it gives as many specific ideas as possible on how organizations can set themselves apart by regularly doing things that will truly WOW their members.

Many of the ideas that are shared in this book aren't new, but they have been updated to make them meaningful in the current membership marketplace. There may also be some ideas and examples in this book that are either the same as, or similar to, information presented in earlier books on the same topics. They are repeated here because they are still applicable in today's challenging member retention environment, and can help reinforce some key points presented in *Retention Wars.*

Some of these ideas will be ideas that have worked for membership organizations throughout the world, others will be ideas that only apply to certain types of organizations in certain specific situations. In all cases they will be ideas that have been used successfully by at least one membership organization.

It is hoped that the information in this book will be of value to all readers. If so, then perhaps this book can help membership organizations do a better job of keeping their members, and adding to their group's financial and human resources.

Readers of this book should take note of those ideas that can be most helpful to their organizations right now. In addition, it is hoped readers will look at some of the ideas that have been included and put them away to use another day, as their organization and their retention challenges change.

A note to readers who are located outside of the United States: many of the ideas, information, and situations in this book are based on what is happening in nonprofit membership organizations located in the United States.

While some of the information (especially the statistical and demographic studies noted) is specific to the U.S., the *concepts* discussed are (presumably) common to most nonprofit membership groups. The experiences of nonprofit membership organizations throughout the world have shown that whether the organization is an all-volunteer group promoting better conditions for the emerging black retail sector in South Africa, a professional women's organization providing retraining to displaced government workers in the former Soviet Bloc countries, or a business association advocating fewer international trade barriers in Latin America, there are common challenges in the areas of member involvement and membership retention. It is hoped that the messages and ideas contained in *Retention Wars* can be "translated" to help all membership organizations, regardless of their location, in their retention battles.

(Author's Note: Although I tried to find ways to relate experiences in a generic manner, I wasn't always able to do that and still get the intent of message across in a meaningful way. So, in Chapter 1, and in a few other instances in this book, you'll find information or situations presented from a first-person perspective. I hope that these passages will add to, rather than distract from, the value of *Retention Wars*.)

Rule Number 1
Learn to Value EVERY Member

In over 30 years of work in organizational management, I've learned a lot of things about membership recruitment and membership retention. Most of these things I've learned by being on the front lines of every organization for which I've ever worked (as a staff professional) or volunteered (as a member). I've been out there, asking people to join, trying to start new chapters, and worrying about whether or not members were going to renew again the next year. Yes, I've seen membership from every level and from every perspective, and I like to think that I've learned a little something from every challenge I've faced. Without question, the most important membership lesson I ever learned came not from my experience as a volunteer, or from my experience as an association executive, or even from my experience as a fundraiser for the Boy Scouts. The most important membership lesson I ever learned came when I was fourteen years old, and the lesson came from my father.

And from a man named Mr. Pete.

When I was growing up, my family owned a carry out store in a very poor part of Washington, D.C. Our store was a small, narrow establishment with eight stools on which customers could sit at the counter. It was a family business in every sense of the words. My mother and father started the business right after World War II. My two brothers and I used to take turns working at the store during the summer, and, to our eternal dread, on alternating weekends during the school year. Saturdays were the worst, because you missed out on the one day you were really free to hang out with your friends or go to the football game at school.

Mr. Pete was an old retired gentleman who lived in the neighborhood near our store. He was one of our most reliable customers. He was also a man of habits. Every day he would come into our store at the same time, shuffling along in his arthritic crouch, leaning on his cane. He was always dressed pretty much the same way, wearing his trademark straw hat, a clean white shirt, pressed dark trousers, and a perfectly placed bowtie. He would stop at the newspaper rack to get his copy of the Washington Daily News, and then he would go over and sit on His Stool. It had to be a very specific stool, not just any stool. It was in a certain place at the counter, and that's where Mr. Pete was comfortable, and that's where he was going to sit. If someone else was sitting in his seat, he'd wait. Often, my father would politely ask other customers if they would mind moving down so Mr. Pete could have his special stool.

After getting settled in, Mr. Pete spread out his paper and got ready for a nice, long luncheon experience. In addition to his daily routine of getting dressed the same way, going to the same place, reading the same paper, and sitting in the same spot, Mr. Pete also ordered the same lunch every day. He ordered the Daily Special. After being served, Mr. Pete would spend the next ten minutes cutting his meal into small pieces, and that routine was followed by about an hour to an hour and a half of Mr. Pete "gumming" his lunch (he had almost no teeth). Every day his bill came to the same amount – two dollars, including his paper.

One Saturday at lunchtime I was busy waiting on customers, feeling sorry for myself about missing another sporting event at the high school, when Mr. Pete came in for his regular lunch. After getting settled in, he was quietly reading his paper while I was running back and forth trying to serve lunches, take money, and generally help my father with the luncheon crowd. As I rushed past Mr. Pete with an arm load of dishes, Mr. Pete very quietly said (in his high pitched voice), "How are you doing, young fellow?"

Well, I was busy, that's how I was doing, and hassled, and really not in a very good mood. I quickly walked past without acknowledging Mr. Pete (or anyone else). I just wanted to get on with my work, and get out of that store as soon as possible.

A short while later, when things had settled down, my father (who had been working back at the grill) came over to me, took me aside, and asked in a very agitated voice "Did you hear Mr. Pete say hello to you a few minutes ago?"

"Yeah," I said, "I heard him, but I was so busy and hassled I just didn't have time to stop and talk."

"When a customer says something to you, you say something back," he told me.

"Dad," I pleaded, "it's only Mr. Pete. For crying out loud, it's just a two-dollar lunch."

That was NOT the right thing to say to my father. And, although I was a "strapping" fourteen-year old, in a flash my father had grabbed me by the collar, practically lifted me off my feet, and dragged me around from behind the counter and out the front door of our store onto the sidewalk. Still holding my collar, my father said, "Look across the street. What do you see over there?"

Parked directly across the street from the front of our store was a brand new, powder blue, early model year 1963 Pontiac Catalina convertible, with white wall tires, a white top, and white interior. It looked like it was about a quarter of a mile long, and it had big fins in the back. It seemed to take up about three parking meters on the street. It was the first brand new car our family had owned in many years, and we had just bought the car a few days earlier.

"I see our new car," I said innocently enough. "What's the point?"

My father said, "The point, Mr. Smart Guy (at least I THINK that's the name he called me), is that Mr. Pete paid for that car."

"What are you talking about?" I asked. "Mr. Pete didn't pay for that car. Mr. Pete never spends more than two dollars any time he comes in here."

My father countered with "O.K., Smart Guy, how many days a week does Mr. Pete come in here?"

"I don't know," I said, "maybe five or six times a week."

"So," my father asked, "how much is that a week?"

"Ten dollars, maybe twelve dollars a week," I said. "Big deal."

"Keep going," my father said. "How much is that in a year?"

"Oh, I don't know, about five hundred or six hundred a year," I said.

"That's right. And how many years do think Mr. Pete has been coming in here, five or six days a week, Mr. Smart Guy?"

"I have no idea," I said.

"Seventeen years," my father said. "That's how long Mr. Pete has been eating lunch in our store. Mr. Pete not only bought that car, he bought the one we had before it, and if I can keep him alive long enough, he'll pay for the next one, too."

That's the day I first learned about the concept of lifetime value.

That's the day I learned, at fourteen years old, how much one satisfied customer can mean to an organization. That's still the best lesson I ever learned about the importance of membership retention, and the need to have a member service philosophy that literally *treasures* every member as a valuable asset.

The concept of the *lifetime value* of a member is nothing new. Membership organizations around the world develop their organizational structure, budgets, programs, and strategic plans around the number of members they anticipate will renew each year. They also count on a certain number of these members participating in the organization's programs and activities, and on these members contributing a certain amount of non-dues revenue via this participation. No, the concept of the lifetime value of a member is nothing new. What IS new is the environment in which organizations are forced to face this challenge of keeping the members they have worked so hard to attract.

If you get nothing else from the book, it is hoped you get a greater appreciation for what each and every member can mean.

Here are some ways to assure that your organization is placing adequate value on every member.

1) If you haven't already done so, calculate the average lifetime value of one member for your organization. It will not only help you appreciate what each member adds to your organization financially, it will also help you in planning your future retention activities. This lifetime value information can show why your organization needs a well-designed and well-implemented retention program.

2) Do a comparison between the amount of money your organization has budgeted for new member recruitment and how much it has budgeted for membership retention (many organizations don't even have a separate line item for membership retention). Once you have calculated the lifetime value of a member, you will see how much more cost-effective it is to retain members than it is to try to replace the members who drop out with new members.

3) Be sure that your organization doesn't "play favorites." It is easy to fall into the trap of making sure that your organization's high profile members receive special attention. These high profile members would include your officers, your Board, your committee

chairs and members, your leaders at the affiliate level, your largest companies, your highest dues payers, your past officers, largest contributors, etc. These are the people and companies who are known to your staff and other leaders as the dedicated and active members. Yes, they do deserve recognition and thanks for their support of your organization, but that doesn't mean that other less active members should get a lower level of service.

4) Personalize your communications with all members as much as you can, given the resources of your organization. People like to be called by name, so use basic mail merging and email merging technologies to personalize your communications. Even if you have a large organization (actually, *especially* if you have a large organization) addressing members in a personalized manner shows that you care about them as individuals.

5) Do periodic surveys of your *least active* members. Asking their opinion is one of the best ways to show that you value their membership.

6) Close the loop on all member communications. Even when a member does nothing more than send in the renewal dues, that activity deserves to be acknowledged. If members think you value them, they will continue giving your organization their loyalty.

It's one thing to say that your organization values every member, but it is another thing to show it. Use all of your resources to let your members know that you appreciate their membership.

Think about it – in every organization there are probably a lot of Mr. Petes.

Rule Number 2
Understand the New Meaning of Involvement

One of the most basic tenants of membership retention has always been "Involved Members Don't Drop Out." The message is clear and simple - if we can get members involved in the organization, the likelihood of their renewing goes up. In fact, the likelihood of members renewing is almost directly proportional to the level of their involvement.

There is no real argument with this theory. It has always been true, and it's true now. That hasn't changed. However, something HAS changed that has a big impact on this concept.

The definition of "involvement" has changed.

When organizational leaders think of their group's "involved" members they tend to think of their leadership – members who get involved in some way in the management of the organization. These involved members would include officers, Board members, committee chairs, committee members, Chapter/affiliate leaders, etc. No question about it, these people are involved, and they're not likely to leave.

But what percentage of an organization's total membership is ever going to serve in one of these leadership roles? 5%? 10%? What about the other 90% of members? Are they going to leave if they don't get "involved?"

Not if organizational leaders change their mindset about the definition of involvement.

In this marketplace, where time is the new currency and everything is measured by the units of time, not of money, getting involved in a membership organization in the traditional way is at least two levels removed from reality for most members. Before they will become involved, they have to become *engaged*. Once they've become engaged, there is at least a *chance* that they will become involved.

Conclusion: organizations need to spend more time trying to get more members engaged, and once that happens then organizations can work on getting them involved.

Here are some ways to get more members engaged in membership organizations.

1) Use technology in as many ways as possible. If members aren't going to attend at the rate that they used to, then they need to be shown that there is value even when they don't physically participate in programs, events, etc. Technology gives organizations

some excellent opportunities to engage a growing number of members.

Some examples include:

a) Taking frequent (short) online surveys
b) Having all educational programs available on web sites
c) Allowing for online registrations and dues payments
d) Setting up listserves and chat rooms for various member segments
e) Allowing for online voting in organizational elections
f) Holding telephone or online focus group activities with newer and less active members

2) Appeal to members to get engaged in ways that take as little time as possible. Break down larger, more time consuming jobs into smaller ones. Most members probably would like to get more involved in their membership organization, but they can't conceive of putting in the kind of time they see organizational leaders commit.

a) Try to estimate exactly how much time a member can expect to have to commit to a specific job. If the time commitment can be broken down into hours per month or week, then the member can make a much more informed decision regarding whether or not to accept the position offered.

b) Give members choices. Instead of "Would you be interested in serving on our committee?" say something like "There are several ways you could get involved in our organization. Given your time constraints, where would you feel most comfortable getting started?"

3) Try to get members engaged in a way that is comfortable for them. Anticipate some of the major concerns that people will have when moving from being a member to being an "active" (in their mind) member. This is especially true when trying to get young people to become engaged in an organization for the first time. According to a study done by a team of demographers in the U.S., most young people want five questions answered before they will commit to taking on a larger role in their organizations. These questions are:

a) What is expected of me?
They want to know what type of commitment they are being asked to make and what the outcome of their time commitment will be. They want to be sure that they are being asked to do something that will be worthwhile, and they want to know what the expectations are of their involvement.

b) What training will I get?

People want to be successful in whatever role they play in the organization. Young people, especially, are concerned that they may not have the experience or training needed to be successful in their volunteer role. Be sure to explain what training or orientation the organization will provide to help them accomplish whatever goal is set for them and their fellow volunteers.

c) How much time is involved?
Specifics are needed here. Don't try to "undersell" volunteer jobs by telling members that it won't be too much of a time commitment. Be honest about the estimated time commitment being requested and let the members make up their own minds based on their priorities.

d) How many others have volunteered?
Young people will be reluctant to become actively engaged in the organization if they think they are going to be part of only a small group of people who have made that commitment. They want to be assured (especially when taking on their first volunteer role) that there will be a support system involved.

e) Has anyone like me volunteered?
Not only do young people want to know if they will be the only ones engaged in this activity or job, they also want to know if any other young

people (or people of a similar background, or color, etc.) have made the same commitment. Of course, this doesn't mean that these people aren't interested in helping the organization, it just means that to get people started in their active roles the organization needs to do everything possible to make them feel comfortable in those roles.

Yes, organizations need to do everything possible to get members involved and engaged. It IS true- the more active and engaged members are, the more chance there is that they will renew their membership. The challenge for organizational leaders today is to understand the new meaning of involvement.

Rule Number 3
Don't Fall Victim to Lag Time

In recent years, input from hundreds of organizations around the world indicates that their most pressing problem is membership retention. It seems that many organizations are doing fairly well in attracting new members but keeping them is another story. Statistics show (not surprisingly) that the greatest number of dropped members each year comes from members who just joined during the previous year. These members joined but never renewed – not even one time!

This statistic was no shock, since it has long been known that new members are among the highest risks for dropping out. Research done by one large (2.6 million member) organization found that this pattern was having a disastrous effect on its struggle to grow. After analyzing all of the aspects of their recruitment and retention efforts, the organization's leaders concluded that the retention problem was caused by three major factors:

1) Many new members signed up because other people in their institution did, and they weren't really committed to the organization and its goals; 2) The "new generation" of members doesn't seem to be as loyal to membership organizations as previous generations; and 3) There has been such an enormous

growth in competition from other organizations, the internet, and time-challenged lifestyles, that it is not reasonable to expect members to stay in an organization if they don't get "involved" during the first year.

While these were all reasonable conclusions, there are still some aspects of this situation that can be addressed and controlled. It was suggested to the organization that they might be overlooking one of the biggest, and the most *easily-corrected*, retention problems. This problem can be summed up in the two words that strike fear into the hearts of membership people everywhere:

LAG TIME!

No, that is not a typographical error. It is not supposed to read "rag time," or any other kind of music. The correct term is **lag** time, and it's causing a lot of organizations to lose a lot of members unnecessarily.

Lag time has been defined as "the time that elapses between the actual completion of a membership application, and the time at which the new member is finally and officially a part of the organization."

Membership managers should write that down, because if it is forgotten, it will come back to haunt them.

In the case of the organization mentioned earlier, follow up was done with a random sampling of their new members, checking to see how long it was from the date of joining (filling out an application) to the time the new member was totally integrated into the organization's system at all levels. That included being accurately listed on the membership records of the local, state, and national organizations (membership is required at all three levels); receiving whatever welcoming/new member communications each level sends to new members; and receiving current information in a real-time manner (vs. having current issues of the organization's publications included in the new member packet).

The organization discovered that in many cases it took anywhere from *six weeks to six months* for new members to reach this point of full inclusion. It was also discovered that it was taking half that amount of time (three weeks to three months) to receive even an *acknowledgement* from all levels of the organization (local, state, and national).

Before thinking "That's ridiculous. That would never happen in a well-managed organization," consider a few things.

1) Don't be so sure. If an organization has an affiliate /chapter system, remember that they are all "guilty by association." Just because one level

(local, state, or national) does timely follow up to new members doesn't mean that the other levels do, too.

2) Exactly when was the application received? Did it sit in a volunteer's or affiliate's office for days (or weeks) before it was forwarded for processing? Better look at that date on the application or check again.

3) If the member joined through the national organization, when did the affiliate get the information and (more importantly) what did they do with it (and how quickly)?

4) What type of follow-up or acknowledgement went out? Who is in charge of "quality control" when it comes to communicating with new members, especially with that first, critical welcoming message?

In addition to making good sense, helping lower dropout rates, meeting member expectations, and adding to the pool of potential leaders, here is another reason (as if any more were needed) why having a systematic, efficient, and timely new member intake program is so important: *the competition already has one.*

This competition isn't just other membership organizations (although many of them now have these systems in place), it is the *private sector*. Virtually every company now has an almost instantaneous follow-up system in place to respond to customers. Can membership organizations make the same claim? Many can't.

Don't make assumptions about the efficiency of organizational partners - find out what's going on. Put a plan together to be certain that whatever the reasons are for losing members, lag time isn't one of them.

Here are fifteen ways to make new member intake efforts successful.

1) Leaders at every level of the organization need to assure that when an application reaches their level, an acknowledgement is sent to the applicant that same day!

2) Have the acknowledgement come from a member. For example, send an email that says something as simple as "Congratulations! I just learned from our headquarters office that you've applied for membership in the XYZ Organization. You've made a great decision, and I hope you get a lot out of your membership. I look forward to meeting you at our next national meeting. Sincerely, Jennifer Jones, National Membership Chair" (or President, etc).

3) Even if the organization has an approval system (i.e. Board acceptance) there should be an acknowledgement of receipt of the application, with a notation that says something like, "As you know, all membership applications must be approved by our Board. We expect the Board to review your application in a few days, and you'll be notified as soon as they have acted. In the meantime, we'd encourage you to visit our web site to start finding out more about how you and your company will benefit from XYZ membership."

4) Work with affiliates to develop a system of immediate follow-up at their levels, too. Sometimes local chapters/affiliates can add a more personal touch by having current members call the new members to welcome them to the organization.

5) Set up an automated message that goes to new members as soon as their information is entered into the membership database. This alleviates the need for someone to send the welcoming messages manually.

6) Use the first follow up contact to gain important additional information about the new member. This is a non-threatening type of message, since the member is already in.

7) Instead of "orienting" new members, interview them. Whether it's in person, via written form, or online, ask new members questions about themselves, rather than spending time telling them about the organization. Based on the responses, set up a series of messages to these members which point out ways they can get what they need through the organization.

8) Set up a system to notify designated current members when a new member who lives or works near them joins the organization.

9) Send a special "gift" to new members as part of their welcoming packet. It can be something as simple as a free publication or even something a little more creative, such as a certificate good for a free cup of coffee at a nearby retail outlet.

10) Be sure to send a copy of any welcoming correspondence, regardless of format, to affiliates. This will show the affiliate that the organization is responsive to new members and will reduce the chances of duplicate messages going to the new members.

11) Make sure affiliates reciprocate by sending copies of their welcoming correspondence to the parent organization.

12) If there is a membership approval process and accompanying waiting period, give new applicants a special temporary member password so they can visit the members-only section of the organization's web site. Once the member is approved make the password permanently active.

13) If the organization has an electronic version of its membership roster that is available on its web site, send new members a note and ask them to check their listing to be sure it's accurate. Get new memberships off to a solid start by showing new members that the organization is committed to quality.

14) Send new members an electronic copy of the organization's logo. Make it easy for the member to forward the logo to a printer or graphic artist so it can quickly and easily be added to stationery, business cards, or advertising copy.

15) Set up a system to automatically send a message to members six months after they join. Have the message be a mini-survey about something important in the profession, industry or community. Make note of new members who don't reply, and do a follow up contact to them.

There is a great challenge – and a great opportunity – to engage new members in the organization in a way that can lead to long-term commitment. Organizations can impress new members with their ability and desire to bring them into the organization quickly and efficiently, or these same organizations can fall victim to the lasting affects of "lag time."

Remember, in membership retention, timing can be everything.

Rule Number 4
Fight Against Identity Theft

Identity theft wasn't a common phrase until a few years ago. It probably has been around for a long time, but was used mostly in relation to the world of sophisticated criminals and the people trying to catch them. Identity theft has now become a huge issue, another example of how technology seems to be able to change everything - except human nature. It seems as though whenever there is something good and useful created, like the incredible opportunities electronic communications provide, there will be some dishonest persons trying to find a way to cheat the system.

In the private sector, identity theft has come to mean a criminal act. In the world of voluntary membership organizations, however, there is a different kind of identity theft going on. This *organizational identity theft* may well be as costly as the criminal kind, if organizations fail to see what's going on and make the necessary changes to deal with it.

What's happening everywhere is that the *image* of voluntary and membership-based organizations has changed, and not necessarily for the better. There are several reasons for this:

1) Bad publicity.

In the past 5-10 years there have been numerous well-publicized scandals involving not-for-profit organizations and their staff and volunteer leaders. While many of these scandals have involved charitable organizations, each incident reflects poorly on all nonprofit and membership-based organizations. If the public thinks that the money they send to nonprofits via dues or contributions is being wasted, stolen, or diverted to the personal use of organizational leaders, then it is only a matter of time before they start withholding their support of, and membership in, these organizations.

2) Political attacks

It may seem like a stretch to say that membership organizations have come under political attacks, but in many ways they have. In virtually every election campaign, and at virtually every level of government (at least in the United States), candidates speak out against the "special interest groups" supporting their opponents. The derogatory term "special interest group" is usually directed at a lobbying group, often one affiliated with a membership organization, such as a trade association or professional society. (Note: It's always interesting to hear a candidate attack these groups when they support the candidate's opponent, yet when these same or similar groups support the candidate they are merely his or her "constituents.")

The fact is, all membership organizations are special interest groups – that's why they were formed, to represent, and give voice to, the interests of various segments of society. Membership organizations advocating the views and beliefs of free people are among the cornerstones of democracies around the world. Unfortunately, many of these organizations have allowed the public to be convinced that carrying out their mission to speak for liked-minded individuals is somehow a negative attribute. The problem is, this image costs these membership organizations support they might otherwise be able to attract and keep.

3) Competition from other sectors

In today's world, many of the products and services that used to be provided solely by membership organizations are now provided by private companies and/or governmental agencies. This has a direct impact on membership retention because, for many years, in order to obtain these products and services, people or companies were required to maintain membership in an organization. Now almost everyone can go directly to the source of the products or services, and eliminate the "middle man" (the membership organization).

(Note: For more on this issue, see Rule 5 - "There are No More Golden Handcuffs")

Are there things that can be done to restore the "identity" of membership organizations, and help them keep the support of their members and contributors? Of course there are.

Changing the Face of an Organization

Let's first look at an example of what some organizations have done to change their image and "rebrand" their organizations.

If most people heard the names "Kiwanis,"Rotary" or "Lions," they would probably think of the generic term "Service Clubs." That's how these organizations have come to be known to the vast majority of people in the United States, and throughout the world. When people think of Kiwanis, or Rotary, or Lions, they might very well conjure up visions of local activities, fund raisers, bull roasts and picnics, floats in local parades, and any number of community service projects. And these images would be correct.

Each of these groups (and hundreds more like them) has a strong tradition - and an indelible image - of community service. What's not as well known as the current image of these groups is their history, and more specifically, their origins.

Rotary (officially known as Rotary International) actually started in 1905 in Chicago as a way for local business leaders to meet and expand their circle of contacts with other business people. The term "Rotary" comes from the fact that the members took turns (rotated) the hosting of their weekly get-togethers.

A few years later, in 1917, another Chicago businessman decided that maybe there was room for other business-based organizations. His existing group, The Business Circle of Chicago, was like Rotary in that it was originally designed to broaden the scope of business contacts for its members. The spin-off group he created eventually became Lions International.

Not too far away, in Detroit, local business and community leaders found that they, too, wanted regular meetings with their peers. They formed what grew into today's Kiwanis Clubs International.

Interesting, isn't it, that these three organizations, which are (deservedly) recognized worldwide for their generosity and community service, all started off as business development organizations? Even today, nearly 100 years after their founding, some of these service clubs maintain membership rules and requirements that harkens back to those early, "special interest" days.

Rotary, for example, still limits membership in its local clubs to a certain number of members per business category. If there is, for example, a secretarial service that wants to become a member of a local club, it can only do so if there are no more than a limited number of other secretarial services already in.

A bad rule? Not necessarily. It's just the way Rotary and some of the other Service Clubs are structured. The point is, Rotary is still designed as a business-based organization, providing business development benefits to its members. Most people never make the connection between Rotary and business development.

What did each of these groups do to go from being identified as just another example of business people trying to gain a competitive advantage towards being identified as an altruistic, community-based service organization?

They changed their image. They rebranded themselves. They created the identity they wanted, and through the years they didn't fall victim to identity theft.

In the case of these three organizations (Rotary, Kiwanis, and Lions), they changed their images through *affiliation.* Each group undertook a specific cause and made it the cornerstone of their organization - their "brand." For Rotary, this became a goal of finding a way to wipe out polio on a worldwide basis. For Lions, it was becoming known for their efforts to aid those with vision defects (i.e. the Lions "eye bank"). Kiwanis is dedicated to the reduction of childhood illnesses, with a special focus on iodine deficiency.

This doesn't mean that every membership organization has to be affiliated with the fight against a universal health problem in order to create or sustain the identity it wants to have with its various publics. Affiliation is only one of the ways organizations can create, or change, and then enhance - and protect - the identity they want.

Here are some suggestions for other ways to guard against identity theft.

a) Whatever the organization's mission or vision is, make sure it is well communicated and well publicized. The ability to create clear, meaningful mission and vision statements will help an organization stand out against others. The organization needs to be consistent with mission and vision statements, and use every form of communication possible to show members that the organization stands for something very worthwhile-something worth supporting again next year.

b) In addition to getting its mission and vision publicized, each organization should find ways to communicate what *values* the organization has. Getting this message out about the organization's values is an excellent way to impact retention, because this will differentiate the membership organization from its for-profit competitors.

c) Identify clearly what the benefits of membership in the organization are, and use these benefits to create targeted "reminder" notices to members throughout the year. Don't wait until renewal time to start trying to convince members that there is enough value in membership to justify rejoining the following year.

d) Create some emotional attachment to the organization while at the same time communicating the tangible benefits of membership. Getting both tangible and intangible member benefits in front of members early in the program year will remind them that membership provides tangible value for the member and his/her employer, and emotional value for being part of something in which the member can believe.

e) Every time a member orders a publication, or registers for a meeting or some other function, add a line in their acknowledgment message that says "Thanks for your publications order. Your order is being shipped tomorrow. Did you know that had you not been a member of our organization these publications would have cost you an additional 20%?"

One aspect of identity theft that can be easily remedied occurs when an organization's image isn't "stolen," but it is actually *given away*. Here an example of an organization giving away its positive image.

A national construction industry trade association was anxious to redesign and rewrite its basic membership literature in order to help the organization stand out in the crowded field of construction associations (there are literally thousands of local, state, and national construction groups in the United States). To get the attention of members and prospective members, the organization believed it needed an effective marketing slogan. They formed a committee of members and staffers to look at possible slogans, and the recommendation that came back from this group was: "The XYZ Association - the best kept secret in the construction industry."

If that was going to be their marketing slogan, they needed to keep looking for a better one. To someone outside of the organization, this slogan basically said, "You probably never heard of us but after you read this material we want you to send us money and join anyway."

What kind of a message is that? Organizations should never want to be "the best kept secret" in their industry or profession or community. Organizations should want to be the best KNOWN organization in their industry or profession or community. They should want to be identified as the leader, not some group that's in hiding. Establishing a positive identity is about getting the organization's message out there, not participating in some witness protection program for nonprofits. Why would any organization want to have a marketing slogan that emphasizes the fact that it isn't very good at getting its message out?

There are already more than enough ways for organizations to become victims of identity theft. They shouldn't be making the situation worse by giving their identity away.

Rule Number 5
There Are No More Golden Handcuffs

Membership retention has always had just as much impact on the success and growth of membership organizations as it does today, but in previous times the challenge of retaining members was somewhat different. A great number of organizations felt secure in their ability to retain members because they had a program, or service, or product that was considered indispensable to its members. In order to continue getting these indispensable products, of course, members had to maintain their membership in the organization. These programs, products, and services were sometimes known as "Golden Handcuffs," meaning that members who participated in these programs were literally handcuffed to the organization and forced to renew because they didn't want to risk losing their eligibility in the programs. Among the programs that fell into this category of "Golden Handcuffs" were insurance programs, certification programs, workers compensation programs, group buying or group discount programs, various professional and business designations, and listings in membership directories.

These programs have been great for the organizations that have provided them. In today's membership retention marketplace, however, there is one small problem: the Golden Handcuffs are disappearing.

As was noted earlier, there is more competition than ever before for members' time and money. Much of that competition is coming from the private sector, the internet, and from other nontraditional sources. The more options people and companies have to obtain programs and services that don't require membership (and accompanying dues costs) in an organization, the less chance there is that they will pay membership dues to gain access to what they want or need.

Here are a couple of examples of the competition membership groups now face from nontraditional sources.

In the past, if individuals or companies wanted to buy insurance, they joined a membership organization to get access to it. In today's market, it is unlikely they'll start their insurance search with nonprofit organizations that require membership. More than likely, they'll start their search with the internet. If individuals or companies want to get exposure to potential customers or clients, it's much more likely that they will develop and market their own web sites than pay to be listed (along with all of their competitors!) on a generic industry or profession website sponsored by a membership organization.

In the past, many membership associations and societies were able to attract and keep members by promising to reduce the "hassle" of dealing with governmental agencies. In addition to the burdensome paperwork requirements, there were the challenges of getting the "run around" when visiting government offices, being put on interminable "hold" when trying to contact government agencies or officials by phone, and standing in seemingly endless lines at government facilities. (Note: In Maryland there used to be a joke that claimed when you entered the Department of Motor Vehicles headquarters office you saw a sign hanging overhead which read "Abandon all hope, ye who enter here.")

While there is no question that dealing with governmental bodies can still be a frustrating experience, even the public/government sector has become a *competitor* for membership organizations. Governmental agencies (at all levels) have learned the value of enhanced customer service. Online accessibility to government forms and information, automated menus to get callers to the appropriate department or person, and fax-on-demand services for thousands of paperwork requirements has made dealing with the government less time consuming and daunting. This means that members and potential members may no longer be willing to pay dues to organizations simply to gain quick access to government-related information. Indeed, going through an organization to obtain this information may, in fact, be viewed as a *slower* way to get what is needed. Why deal with the "middleman" – the membership organization - when you can go directly to the source with confidence that you'll get what you want?

A quick word about "members-only" programs. Just because a product or service or program is designated "members-only," that doesn't make it an exclusive or unique product. It just means that in your organization, only members can get it. It doesn't eliminate the basic fact that people who are not members may very well be able to get it through other sources.

Does this mean that there are NO Golden Handcuffs left?

Not necessarily. In some industries, professions, and communities there are still programs, products, and services for which the organization has little or no competition.

The problem isn't the present - it's the future. What will happen to an organization that depends heavily on Golden Handcuff programs if the Golden Handcuff programs disappear?

There are three basic techniques that can be used to overcome the loss of Golden Handcuffs:

1) Have a *plan* for dealing with it.

2) Be able to identify, and effectively market, what makes your organization *unique*.

3) Use the organization's *competitive advantage* effectively.

Here are some examples of how to use each of these techniques.

1) Have a plan for dealing with it.

Case Study: How One Organization Faced the "No More Golden Handcuffs" Scenario

The South Dakota Ranchland Association (SDRA)* is, by almost every measurement, a successful organization. It has grown almost every year, despite an actual decrease in the number of ranchers in their state. It is widely recognized as one of the largest, most influential agricultural organizations in the state. It has won awards and recognitions from its national affiliate, in categories such as program development, staff performance, and membership retention.

So what was the problem? Actually, there wasn't one. In fact, one of the main reasons SDRA was so successful was because of its cornerstone Golden Handcuffs benefit - its insurance program.

For twenty years, SDRA had been able to attract, and keep, a growing number of members because of its close relationship with the insurance company that managed the SDRA insurance programs. The "golden" aspect of the insurance program, of course, was the

not the actual name of the organization

fact that in order to get and keep the insurance coverage, members had to join *and maintain* their SDRA membership.

Through the marketing and sale of various types of insurance, SDRA attracted hundreds of new members each year. Insurance agents were actually responsible for recruiting or referring almost half of the new members that joined SDRA each year. This steady stream of new members and policyholders enabled SDRA and the insurance company to work in a mutually beneficial way year after year.

In addition to attracting new members through this source, SDRA was able to attain extremely high member retention rates because of the continued SDRA membership clause in the policies that the insurance company sold. Once a quarter SDRA provided the insurance company with the names of those SDRA members who held insurance policies but had not yet renewed their membership in SDRA. The insurance company then sent a friendly reminder to these members stating that in order to keep the insurance the members also needed to keep an SDRA membership. Most of them took the reminder seriously and sent their renewal payment to SDRA in a timely manner.

Then came the "good news-bad news" message from the head of the insurance company. The good news was that the insurance company was going to continue making membership in SDRA a requirement for purchasing insurance. The bad news: starting with the beginning of the next calendar year, the *continuous* SDRA membership requirement would no longer apply. If policyholders did not renew with SDRA, they would no longer get the "reminder" notice from the insurance company.

Rather than panicking, SDRA leaders decided to put a plan together to overcome the loss of their greatest Golden Handcuff. They realized that they basically had a year to prepare for the change, and their leadership (staff and volunteer) dedicated time – and money – to this challenge.

First, they decided that whatever the outcome, the challenge of losing this major retention tool would be approached in a positive way. There was no name calling, finger pointing, or throwing arms up in despair. In fact, SDRA started right away to view the changes in the insurance program as a focal point for re-evaluating, and improving, many of their membership development and member relations activities. They created a member/staff retention committee, and this group put a detailed plan of action together. The plan had several key components, but the overall objective of the plan was simple and straightforward: do everything possible to reduce the impact of the insurance changes on membership retention.
To help both staff and volunteer leaders become committed to their individual and collective roles in

keeping SDRA retention rates high, the organization adopted a slogan that was kept in front of their leaders at all times:

"Make membership desired, not just required"

This simple statement said it all. SDRA had a year to convince members that even if they don't <u>have</u> to renew their membership (to keep the insurance) they should <u>want</u> to renew it because of the overall value of SDRA membership. SDRA's plan to make membership desired not required consisted of the following elements:

a) Partnering with the insurance company to be certain the changes in the program were communicated in the best way possible to limit the retention impact for SDRA.

Both parties still had a major stake in continuing to attract new clients and new members through the new agreement, and they didn't want to ruin a 20-year relationship by sending mixed messages to their mutual customers/members. The insurance company and SDRA worked hard to assure that the manner in which policyholders were notified of the change did not in any way *encourage* policyholders to drop their SDRA membership. The wording of all information regarding the changes was to be reviewed by both the insurance company and SDRA leaders.

A key element of this partnership was the synchronizing of the methods each organization was using to answer customer/member questions about the changes in the membership requirements. It was important to avoid members getting one explanation from the insurance company and a different explanation from SDRA leadership. Guidelines for answering questions about the changes were written out and distributed to all staffers and leaders, along with an actual script of what to say and answers to the most likely questions staffers would be asked.

b) Creating an enhanced customer-friendly environment within SDRA.

A staff Task Force was created to identify the most important aspects of a top-level customer/member service system, and to evaluate SDRA's current operations in these key areas. Then the Task Force was assigned to make recommendations on how to move from the current level to the desired level of performance. These recommendations included such things as ongoing member/customer service training for all staffers, a permanent customer service staff committee, the establishment of measurement criteria for customer service activities, a revised orientation program for new employees, and increased staff discretion and authority to deal with member service issues.

c) Initiating a targeted public relations effort to remind members of the other (non-insurance) benefits of SDRA membership

Rather than waiting until the renewal notices were sent and hoping (praying) that members would renew, SDRA realized that there was a full year to get its message of value across to its members before the notices of the insurance requirement changes were sent. SDRA set up a system to rate the "at risk" factors of its members. It identified the member segments *most likely* to drop out once the new insurance rules were in place, and designed a series of messages aimed specifically at that group.

Of course, SDRA leaders wanted all of their members to renew, but they realized that with limited time and limited money they had to set priorities. While their core membership consisted of fulltime ranchers, this group of members was least likely to drop out because they were (in most cases) long-time members who were dedicated to SDRA for reasons other than just the insurance rates.

The most vulnerable groups of members fell into three basic categories: those members who had been in SDRA for several years but only sent their renewal payments in when the insurance company's reminders (threats of cancellation) were received; those members who had been members for several years and renewed on time but never participated in any SDRA activity or program other than insurance; and new members, those who joined SDRA the previous year and had not yet gone through a renewal cycle.

SDRA leaders started communicating with these at-risk members first. They then identified and rated other segments and designed a series of contacts with each of these groups. The messages to this most vulnerable group didn't consist of a series of "please don't drop out just because you can" or anything like it. The messages were focused and positive. Knowing that these targeted members were essentially in SDRA to save money on their insurance, SDRA began sending them information on other ways to save money (through other affinity programs, discounts with various suppliers throughout the state, etc.). These messages were followed by a series of testimonial-type messages that quoted SDRA members talking about how they had received value through SDRA in many ways.

Finally, SDRA offered a series of incentives for this group of potential drops to renew. These incentives included reduced dues for early renewal and additional cost-saving opportunities (through coupons and vendor promotions) for renewing within the allotted renewal period.

d) Streamlining administrative procedures associated with membership renewal.

SDRA worked with its local chapters get all new member and renewal information processed by the state organization instead of the chapters. While it took some convincing of local leaders to make this happen, the benefit of the new system was soon apparent to everyone. It decreased the lag time (as described in Chapter 2) associated with new member applications and follow up; it enhanced coordination of the welcoming and retention messages being sent from the state organization and the chapters; it gave the administrative support staff at the local level more time to be in direct contact with late payers and at-risk members; and it meant one less level of the organization handling cash, checks and credit cards, since all payments would now go directly to a bank lock box rather than someone's "IN" box.

SDRA also added online options for both new members and renewing members, something SDRA had not offered before because not all chapters charged the same amount. Again working closely with chapter leaders, SDRA was able to work out a simplified dues structure that allowed chapters to maintain their income levels while making the membership application process less confusing for the prospective or renewing member.

e) Gaining increased commitments from volunteer leaders.

The credibility of the volunteer and staff leaders in SDRA would play a critical part in the battle to overcome the loss of this most important Golden Handcuff program. SDRA knew that it was important for its leaders to be as visible as possible during the transition months (and this first round of renewals) when SDRA membership would, for the first time ever, no longer be required to maintain insurance coverages. It was also important for these leaders to be vocal, as well as visible. They had to be able to articulate the changes and encourage members to renew, they had to be accurate in explaining the changes, and they had to be careful not to look and sound as though they wanted to blame all of the changes on the insurance company.

At the state level, the Board of Directors developed a checklist of ways that Board members could make an impact on membership during this transition year. The SDRA President redesigned the quarterly Board meeting agendas to include time set aside at each meeting for a special report on the progress of the retention plan. Following the overall plan review, the President then asked each Board member to report on his/her membership related activities since the last meeting. While this might seem like a lot of pressure to put on Board members, it really was a sign to everyone - Board members, staff, chapter leaders, and the general membership - that the President and the Board were going to lead by example in this effort.

Among the activities on the Board Involvement Checklist were:

-Recruiting 3-4 new members (to replace the potential drops)
-Contacting chapter leaders to offer assistance in Chapter retention activities
-Helping Chapter Presidents identify and recruit strong Membership Committee Chairs
-Helping staff SDRA booths at state and county fairs and other agricultural events
-Attending Chapter Board meetings to answer questions and help Chapter leaders feel more comfortable explaining the insurance changes to other members
-Making personal contacts with late renewals and asking them to reconsider their decision to drop out
-Writing "testimonial" letters to members who were thinking of dropping out

All of these plan elements had numerous specific activities attached to them. Staff, and where appropriate, volunteers, were assigned to carry out each plan element. While no plan is 100% successful, SDRA's leaders know that without their focused retention plan being in place and actively implemented, the loss of members would have been much greater.

2) Be able to identify, and effectively market, what makes your organization *unique*.

Golden Handcuff programs are being taken from membership organizations because they are readily available through other sources, including many sources which didn't exist until a few years ago. The best way to fight this battle is to look for an opportunity. to focus on whatever it is that makes the organization truly unique. Organizations need to keep away from having their programs, products, and services viewed as commodities, things members can get from any number of sources and at varying prices.

Here are a few suggestions on the types of programs/services that membership organizations should consider highlighting when trying to convince members of the value of renewing their memberships.

a) Representation/advocacy

In some organizations this might be called government relations, or lobbying, or something similar, depending upon the type of organization. It's really the same benefit regardless of the title given to it. This is one aspect of membership organizations that makes them truly unique. In fact, in many organizations, it's the reason the organization was created.

Organizing people/companies/institutions into voluntary organizations has its roots in the history of virtually all successful democracies (See Chapter 4 on Identity Theft). Someone, or some group, recognizes that there is a need that isn't being filled, or a point of view or a belief that isn't being heard. Voluntary organizations are formed to give "voice" to a specific point of view. This age-old concept of strength in numbers is one thing that the internet and private providers of products and services can't duplicate or replace.

Whatever the purpose of the organization, its willingness and ability to speak on behalf of the members (collectively) is a powerful message and a powerful reason to renew. Ironically, it is also somewhat of a paradox in terms of being a member benefit. The fact is, the more members/supporters an organization has, the more vocal and powerful it can be in representing its members. However, part of the way a group attracts members is through its reputation of being effective in representing its constituency. In short, an organization's current membership size is also one of its best recruitment and retention tools.

People want to affiliate with a group that is going to give their viewpoints the best chance of being heard. That means there is, in every sense of the words, real strength in numbers. This message of being able to represent a viewpoint and actually make changes in a profession, industry, or community is something that needs to be highlighted in retention efforts.

Representing members/supporters effectively to their various publics is one program that cannot be turned into a commodity. It's what makes membership organizations unique, and it IS a reason to renew (if marketed effectively).

b) Affinity

In today's membership environment, people would rather talk to each other than to an organization. That means that they want to communicate with people or companies or institutions that believe as they do, work in a setting like theirs, and face the same day-to-day challenges they face. They don't want to talk just to a staff person who works for a membership organization. The key to using affinity as a reason for members to renew is to highlight not the fact that the organization shares their challenges or beliefs, but that the organization is a *catalyst for putting them together with other people or companies or institutions who share their challenges and beliefs.*

While the whole definition of "networking" has changed, the concept of connecting with like-minded people is still something that people value. Membership organizations need to let their members know that no private entity can guarantee that they will be able to put members in touch with others who have true empathy for them and their situation. Membership organizations can make this guarantee, because affinity is one of the reasons they were created in the first place.

c) Proprietary Products, Services, and Programs

As was noted earlier, although there are few generic programs left that have no competition, there are still some very specialized programs that are truly difficult to access without being part of a membership organization. Not many, but some. Organizations that have one (or more) of these types of programs should highlight those benefits as much as possible to retain members.

Some of these unique programs are programs that were started by the organization, and the organization has retained exclusive rights to them. These might include certification or accreditation programs, training programs, and statistical programs. Even organizations that have these unique programs/products/services can't wait until renewal time to remind members that if they drop out of the organization they will no longer have access to these unique programs. This message has to be communicated on an ongoing basis throughout the year.

3) Use your *competitive advantage* effectively.

It is sometimes hard for a volunteer-based membership organization to understand how it could possibly have any competitive advantage over some of the huge, multi-national business conglomerates with which they now compete for the time and attention of their members and prospects. Yet there is an aspect of retention marketing that provides that advantage to membership organizations, IF they recognize it and IF they use it effectively. That advantage is the built-in **customer loyalty** of the members.

The fact that members have already purchased something from the organization - their membership - means that the organization now has what every retailer, wholesaler, marketer, and advertiser dreams about – the proverbial "captive" market. Not captive in the sense that they HAVE to buy any more of the organization's product or services, but captive in the sense that by joining the organization they have given permission for the organization to communicate with them. What the organization does with this permission to communicate will determine the success of its retention efforts.

In general, members want their chosen organization to succeed. They don't expect the organization to provide for their every need, but in the areas that are within the scope of the organization's purposes, if all else is equal, they will usually want to do business with their membership organization. Some members, will, in fact, participate in programs and services out of a feeling of obligation or commitment. While organizations would never want to exploit this feeling, they do want to use it to solidify membership retention.

Be careful not to take this customer loyalty for granted. Always keep on the look out for new ways to engage even more members. Put systems into place that assure the organization is cross-selling products, services, meetings, affinity programs, and other organizational benefits. Whenever a member participates in one aspect of the organization be sure to offer a chance to participate in another benefit.

There may be very few traditional Golden Handcuff programs left for some organizations, but that doesn't mean those organizations have to lose members because of it. Organizations that focus on making membership in the organization desired, and not just required, will be surprised how many "golden" retention opportunities are still out there.

Rule Number 6
Make an Accurate Gap Analysis

In recent years **diversity** has become a catch phrase
for thousands of membership organizations. "We need
to be more diverse;" "We need to be more
representative of our community;" "We need to reach
out to a more diverse group of prospective members."
These are the slogans that have been heard over and
over again within the leadership of membership
organizations. It's not just in the United States, either.
In Australia, for example, there is a growing sense of
urgency among nonprofit groups to attract more people
with culturally and linguistically diverse backgrounds.

Certainly, there is nothing wrong with this emphasis on
attracting a culturally-diverse membership. However,
even though changing demographics mandate that
attracting these culturally-diverse people will be
necessary for the very survival of some organizations,
there needs to be a greater awareness of what *types* of
diversity are causing the greatest challenges - and also
the greatest opportunities.

When people think of diversity in relation to
membership organizations, the most basic types of
diversity that come to mind are race, culture, and
gender. The desire to broaden their membership base
and attract these diverse groups has encouraged
membership organizations to determine where their
membership base has identifiable **gaps**. These gaps
include racial gaps, cultural gaps, and gender gaps.

There is, however, another measurement of diversity that is creating an even greater challenge for membership organizations, and even greater gaps. The biggest challenge most organizations face today is the **generation** gap.

Generational diversity is certainly not a new phenomenon, but the 21st century has brought it into greater focus. Although this generation gap affects organizations around the world, perhaps the most profound effect is being felt in membership organizations in the United States. Many membership groups are having at least minimal success in attracting younger people to membership in their groups, but they are having an *incredibly difficult time keeping them.* In order to retain a generationally-diverse membership, organizations will have to be more focused, more diligent and more flexible than ever before.

Identifying the Generational Traits

There have been numerous studies done and articles (and books) written about the differences in the various generations in society at this point in the early 21st century. In the U.S. there is even some disagreement about *how many* distinct generations are currently living and working in society. For purposes of focusing on how to develop a retention system that will be effective in getting all of these generations to maintain their membership, this discussion will be based on the findings in several studies, but primarily one done by the Foundation of the American Society of Association Executives (ASAE).

In the ASAE study, four distinct generations were identified. These were:

Silents-people born in the period from @ 1930-1945. These people have some memory of World War II and the Great Depression, but reached adulthood just after that era.

Baby Boomers-people born from @1946-1964, the largest generation in American history. These people tended to be the sons and daughters of the men and women of the World War II generation (the generation prior to the Silents)

Generation X- those born from @ 1965-1980. These people were the first generation of Americans likely to grow up in a household with two working parents (or, in many cases, a single-parent home).

Millennials-those born after 1980. This is the first generation of Americans to grow up with computers and the internet as part of their daily lives. This is also the first group of Americans to reach adulthood in the 21st century.

While these generational descriptions apply to people in the United States, there are probably similar trends occurring in other countries.

The Differences

ASAE's study contained an in-depth look at the basic characteristics of each generation. Here is a condensed version of some of the findings of the study.

The Silent Generation

This generation is the one that has carried on many of the traditions of the World War II generation. They tend to have a high degree of respect (even reverence) for people in positions of authority. They are extremely loyal, with many working for the same company or institution for their entire careers. They view leadership as a hierarchy, meaning that people need to "pay their dues and work their way to the top" of the organization, usually through some type of organization chart. Authority and decision-making flowed from the top down. This is also the generation that is least familiar with, and least comfortable with, new technologies (some Silents may have grown up in households with no telephone).

Baby Boomers have been a transitional generation in almost every way. This is the generation of the flower children and their vow to "change the world." Their goal was to drive as hard as possible to get to the top, because that's how to get the power to make changes. Their view of authority was that the person who worked the hardest (i.e. put in the most hours) would attain leadership in the organization. This evolved into what has been described as a love-hate relationship with authority. That means Baby Boomers love authority when they have it, and hate it when they don't. This is also the group that supported decision-making by consensus, which emphasizes allowing all stakeholders to have equal input in important decisions.

Generation Xers tend to be more independent than the previous generations. Part of this is because they grew up in households with two working parents, and were often on their own. Part of it is because they (at least those in the latter half of this generation) were also among the first Americans to use computers extensively. Generation Xers believe that just putting in hours to get to the top (see: Baby Boomers) isn't necessarily the best way to live. They want some balance in their lives, and are the generation that institutionalized such workplace concepts as flex time, day care, and job sharing. Leadership, in their opinion, should be based on ability, not seniority. The most competent people should be the ones in leadership positions.

Millennials are a somewhat more difficult group to analyze, if only because it isn't known what the outer-limit (age wise) of this group is going to be-they are still a work-in-progress. The ASAE study did determine that this group may be a throwback to the Silents in that they seem to have a healthy respect for authority. They believe that leadership should be based on who is best able to help the organization accomplish its goals. They tend to see things with a clearer overall vision, focusing on the long-range outcome. They are the first generation to grow up with the internet, with its worldwide, 24-hour communication capabilities, and endless options on just about everything. This has created a generation with a much more global outlook on things. After all, on the internet there are no geographic boundaries, and there is no discrimination, because on the internet there is no black or white, fat or thin, physically challenged, etc.

What does all of this have to do with membership retention?

Plenty.

Due to the differences noted above, each of these generations tends to look at membership organizations differently. Marilyn Moats Kennedy, noted author and lecturer, has developed a comparison of membership/involvement attitudes among these generations. Here is what she discovered about these distinct groups.

ATTENDANCE

There were some marked differences in each generation's view of what was traditionally thought of as the most basic form of involvement – just showing up!

The older generations (Silents and Baby Boomers) had a pretty simple view: What's the sense of joining an organization if you aren't going to participate? These generations were used to going to meetings on a regular basis.

Generation Xers, however, are much more sporadic in their attendance. Sometimes they attend, sometimes they don't. It depends upon what else is going on in their lives and what their priorities are. Remember, these are also the people more likely to have a working spouse, day care obligations, etc.

Millennials have an even more distant view of attending meetings and functions. Their basic question is "What's the purpose? What does the function/meeting have to do with accomplishing the organization's goals (or my goals)?"

NETWORKING

Networking is perhaps the most frequently cited reason people give for joining an organization, and is perhaps the most frequently mentioned benefit of membership in marketing materials developed by membership organizations. However, different generations have different ideas about what networking really means.

For Silents and Baby Boomers, networking means person-to-person contact. When they think of networking, they think of attending meetings and functions, shaking hands with people and exchanging business cards, etc.

It's completely different for Xers and Millennials. Mention networking to them, and their thoughts go immediately not to a meeting, but to a computer! Their idea of networking is sending emails and visiting chat rooms.

(Here's an idea: go into a neighborhood bookstore and ask the staffers working there if they carry any books on "Networking." Take note of where they go to find a networking book. The chances are they will go to the part of the store that has books on how to set up and run a *computer network*. It's doubtful that any of the books in the bookstore's Networking Section have anything to do with interpersonal communications, which is what networking is really all about).

PARTICIPATION

In addition to having differing ideas about something as basic as just showing up at meetings, each generation has a different way of identifying what they want - and expect - out of their participation.

The older generations participate because of the networking opportunities. To these members, the ability to interact with others who have similar interests or challenges is one of the basic reasons to join or stay in an organization. When deciding whether or not to attend a function or get involved in a leadership position, one of the first things these Silents and Boomers want to know is who *else* will be attending the function or meeting. Are these the people with whom I want to affiliate? How many are coming? How can I get involved in the meeting in a way that will make my attendance more productive and meaningful?

The younger generations of Xers and Millennials see participation in almost an opposite way. Their chief concern isn't who will be there and what will happen at the meeting or function. Instead, their biggest concern is knowing what they will be able to **take away** from the meeting. Whether the meeting or event is a formal continuing educational offering, a community action meeting, or a trade show, their primary concern is the educational value of the event. What did I learn that I can use in my everyday world?

LEADERSHIP/INVOLVEMENT

It is hard enough to get members to participate at any level, much less at the leadership level. Organizations have to point out, and communicate, the value of this enhanced level of participation before members will be willing to get more involved. Communicating the value of participation becomes even more difficult when different generations are involved.

Silents and Boomers participate in membership organizations because they want their voices - or the voices of their employers or companies or institutions - to be heard. They want to be certain that, whenever the organization is formulating policies, their input is included in the decision-making process. To these older generations, it is worth the time and effort it takes to get involved with an organization if that time and effort will help get their point of view adopted or at least considered by the organization. Some members will serve in a leadership group (such as a Board of Directors) for several years just to assure that at some point they will be President or Chair, and have influence over the activities of the organization. Having a "seat at the table" is very important to these demographic groups.

Xers and Millennials, on the other hand, don't feel that they can commit the kind of time it takes to get into a position of leadership or authority, yet they still want to have their input into what the organization is doing. So, if they won't show up, is there any way to gain this access to the decision-making process? Sure there is. They can pay for the access. They can make a donation, join at a higher level, sponsor an event or program, and raise the perceived stature in the organization of themselves and/or their company/institution. This pay for access isn't another sign that younger generations don't have the same commitment and concern for their organizations as older generations do. It's just a different way of achieving the same goal.

What all of this means in terms of membership retention is that there is no longer any one technique that will work to get all of these diverse generations motivated, involved, and engaged at the same level. It means that, in order to keep these members at a high rate, organizations will have to create some specialized and targeted communications to get across the message of why members need to be involved. Knowing the differences in these generations allows modern organizations to analyze those differences, identify the gap between what these generations want from an organization and what the organization currently offers, and then set out to develop methods to bridge this generation gap.

Here are some specific suggestions.

1) The **Silents** present somewhat of a dilemma for many organizations. These older members can be among the most valued and experienced in an organization (often a core part of the leadership), and organizations want to do everything possible to keep these members who have meant so much. On the

other hand, this can be a group that is somewhat resistant to change since they grew up in an era of reverence for authority and belief in hierarchies. This group tends to be less comfortable with new technologies, the same technologies organizations are now turning to in order to engage and keep members. These members may already be getting the feeling that they are being forced out of their organizations because many of these organizations' efforts are being geared toward meeting the needs of the newer generations.

One way to engage and involve these older members is to use them as a bridge between other generations. These older members have been active for many years, and can bring a sense of reason to disputes among younger generations. They can engage younger members by asking them to help develop programs and communications systems to allow for a smoother transition in organizational leadership.

Silents can serve effectively as focus group facilitators. This allows them to use their stature as senior members to call younger members together and get information that the organization can use to further involve these other generations in the organization's programs. In addition to keeping the Silents engaged, these focus groups are also an effective way to engage the younger participants.

Silents can be asked to serve as liaisons to other organizations. Every group has a number of partner organizations with which they want to establish and maintain a relationship. Older members bring experience and credibility to their role as liaisons, they bring useful information back to their organization, and they can stay involved without committing a large amount of time.

Organizations frequently use their Silents by assigning them as "mentors" for younger members. This is certainly a legitimate way to keep older members engaged. They have a lot experience and knowledge to impart, and they enjoy helping younger people succeed.

There is an aspect to this mentoring relationship that should be noted, however. Not all younger members (especially the millennials) will necessarily accept mentoring if it is based solely on the ages of the participants. In a workshop with a panel of Millennials that was held at an ASAE conference, a typical mentoring program was described to the panel. The panelists were asked if they felt a mentoring program would be helpful in getting them started in their respective career fields, and the corresponding membership organizations. One of the participants made an enlightening comment. "I think the general idea of mentoring is fine," he said, "but I don't know if I want to be mentored by someone who is going to tell me how he or she did things 25 or 30 years ago. I might be better off being mentored by someone starting his or her *second* year of membership. That person can help me avoid some of the mistakes he or she might have made when he or she was new to everything."

Some excellent food for thought.

2) The **Baby Boomer** generation is frequently the predominant generation in membership organizations. These are the members that are ascending to the top levels of leadership, or have just finished going through many of these leadership positions. They have been around their organizations for a number of years, and still have several years of membership left before retiring and leaving the organization, *if* organizations can keep them engaged.

Baby Boomers tend to be concerned about "making their mark" in membership organizations. Recognition for their contributions is very important to them. Organizations should give timely and appropriate recognition to this group, remembering to reward participation, not just leadership. This need for impact makes Boomers excellent candidates to serve on committees or Boards that are involved in charitable activities, scholarship programs, and foundations. Boomers make excellent fundraisers, especially when they know that their ability to raise money will be directly related to the recognition they'll get for helping the organization accomplish its goals.

Boomers (in addition to Silents) can also make excellent mentors. Some of the older Boomers are nearing retirement age, and they are anxious to feel that their input still has value in an organization.

Both Boomers and Silents can be used effectively in helping the organization do its strategic and long-range planning. This allows them to use their experience to discuss issues and trends, and allows them to feel as though the plan they develop will in some way be their legacy for the younger generations of members.

3) Engaging **Generation Xers** requires flexibility and creativity. As these members move into an organization's leadership, they are ready to make changes and help the organization answer the challenges of the 21st century. Since this group comes with a more independent point of view, they are open to new ideas and often want to be the leaders of cultural change in an organization.

Xers are excellent at helping organizations diversify. They grew up during the era of vast demographic changes, and can be more understanding of the perspectives of minority groups. They are comfortable approaching non-traditional partners and establishing contacts with minority organizations. They are somewhat more secure in engaging diverse peoples in discussions because they have grown up in an environment where they don't have to stop and think of whether or not their verbal and body language is "politically correct."

Xers want choices (this was the generation that invented flex time). They need to be given options on ways to participate in organizational activities. This might include payment options on dues, the ability to use credit cards for just about everything (including dues), "cafeteria-style" memberships that allow them to pay for only those services they utilize, etc. This desire for flexibility carries over to their view of serving in leadership roles. They are reluctant to commit to years of working their way up through committees and Boards to gain top-level leadership positions.

To engage Xers more fully, organizations should be flexible. Don't let traditional organization charts and leadership ladders be barriers to member involvement. Make room for alternative organizational structures and concepts such as job-sharing and term limits.

4) **Millennials** will present some interesting challenges for membership organizations. To get them engaged, the use of technology is virtually a requirement. They will assume that any type of participation - joining , renewing, ordering, communicating, etc.- will have an online option. These members will be more likely to participate in a chat room than go to a committee meeting, so perhaps online meetings will encourage them to serve on committees in the first place.

Millennials like to see activity and want things to move quickly. To get them engaged, try getting them to work on task forces or ad hoc committees, entities that have specific time frames and specific outcomes. Since their focus is on what can be achieved, Millennials can be used to create alternative (non-traditional) solutions to organizational problems. Doing frequent, short, online surveys can get them interested in other organizational activities.

Generational gaps have a great many causes, but there are also a number of ways to deal with them. Understanding what each generation of members wants, and giving them the opportunity to participate in a manner that is comfortable for them, can close those gaps.

Rule Number 7
You Can Overcome Apathy Through Empathy

What's the matter with members today?

If that question sounds familiar, it may be because it paraphrases a song from the musical "Bye Bye Birdie," a Broadway show that was popular at the height of the Baby Boomer generation. The song to which it refers is called "Kids," and those who remember the song know that the chorus goes: "Kids, I don't know what's wrong with these kids today. Kids! Who can understand anything they say? Why can't they be like WE were, perfect in every way? Oh, what's the matter with kids today?"

The reason reference is made to that song is because when it was originally written and performed (in the late 1950's), the "kids" to whom it referred were the Baby Boomers, who in this song were the target of the lament of the older generations (the World War II and Silent generations). The words to this song point out that every generation seems to think that the next generation is not as involved, not as concerned, not as *good* as their generation. This perception often flows over from society in general into membership organizations. Organizations are always attempting to get more members involved, yet things seem to be going in the wrong direction. These newer generations of members just don't seem to be as interested in doing the work of the organization as the generations before them.

What's the problem with today's members? Why does it seem that they don't participate as much as previous generations? The most logical explanation would be that they don't have the time to participate the way previous generations of members did, but that doesn't make sense. They have the same 24 hours that everyone else has, so they don't actually have *less* time.

If it's not time, maybe it's – APATHY.

That's the word that is often used for this lack of participation. The perceived problem with these new generations of members is they just have too much apathy. Apathy is defined in the dictionary as "lack of interest; indifference." That about sums up these newer generations, doesn't it?

Or does it?

Maybe it just SEEMS that that younger members don't care and don't want to get involved. According to a study done by the Independent Sector (Washington, D.C.) and published in their annual edition of *Giving and Volunteering in America,* 89% of American households DO contribute either time or money to some nonprofit organization each year. What's even more revealing is the fact that an astounding 44% of the adults (over 18) questioned said that they had spent at least *some time* in the past year volunteering for an organization.

Wait a minute. It's hard to find any single *organization* that has a participation rate of its members/supporters that comes anywhere near 44%. It's difficult to believe that 44% of the entire adult population of the United States is giving some time - even a minimal amount of time - to a nonprofit in any given year.

Here are some statistics from that study that are even more enlightening. The survey went on to ask those 56% who said they *didn't* give any time at all to a nonprofit, "Why not? Why didn't you give even one hour to participate in a nonprofit last year?"

The number one reason given *wasn't* "I didn't have the time" (that was number two). The number one reason respondents gave for not participating was "No one asked me."

One more interesting piece of information from that survey: Of the 56% who said they didn't participate because no one asked them, 71% said if someone HAD asked them to get involved, they would have said "Yes!"

These statistics seem a little difficult to believe. Organizations are constantly asking members to get involved, to help the organization, to give just a few hours of their time. Organizations are asking members to get involved, but the members say "No one asked me."

Maybe what these members are saying is "No human being who really understands my situation ever told me why I should give up my precious time to be involved in the organization."

Maybe the answer to overcoming the perceived apathy of members is just a few *letters* away.

Maybe the best way to overcome the **apathy** is through **empathy**.

Isn't it interesting how close those words are? Apathy (disinterest) can be overcome with empathy (understanding another's feelings or motives). But it's not enough just to have empathy. Organizations need to have, or create, "membership empathy."

Membership empathy means that members *believe* the organization understands their situation. What's the difference between *empathy* and *membership empathy*? Having empathy is a characteristic - you possess it or you don't. Membership empathy is a skill - you can communicate it or you can't.

To get more members involved, and retained, organizations have to first establish that they truly understand their members' concerns about time commitments. In order to overcome these concerns, organization need to worry less about getting members involved and more about getting them engaged.

Organizations know that members are time-challenged (empathy) so they need to find volunteer jobs that don't take a lot of time. Perhaps there needs to be an emphasis on developing limited-time task groups instead of committees. Maybe organizations need to use teleconferencing and audio programs more frequently. Members, at least the younger ones, are comfortable with electronic communications (empathy), so organizations should take online member surveys and develop targeted chat rooms to get them engaged. Organizations know that members will get involved if they are asked appropriately, so perhaps organizations need to do away with generic "calls for volunteers" and get current leaders to ask specific people to take on specific roles in the organization.

Apathy is something with which every organization has to deal. If organizations can have empathy for members, and *communicate that empathy* effectively, they have a chance of getting members engaged. If members are engaged and given appropriate recognition and acknowledgement for that engagement, there is a better chance of getting them involved.

What's the matter with members today? Not a thing. We just need to motivate them out of their *apathy* through *empathy*.

Here are some things organizations can do to communicate empathy to their members.

a) Have staff members spend a day with one of the organization's members. Better yet, have them spend several days with several members from different membership segments. Let them learn to see the members' world, and then try to determine how the organization fits into that world.

b) If spending a day with a member is not practical, here's an alternative that one construction association used. They asked a member to address their headquarters staff at a full staff meeting. The member selected was not the organization's president or an officer. In fact, the member was not involved in any way in the leadership of the organization. He was specifically chosen because he was not a leader, and because his company met most of the characteristics of an "average" member of the organization (i.e. size, number of employees, etc.).

The member was asked simply to tell the organization's staff what a typical day was like for him, starting from the time he left his home in the morning until the time he got home in the evening. He told the staff about being on his cell phone in his truck on the way to his office, checking to see if crews showed up on jobs; he told of going to his office to face the paperwork needed to gain permits and comply with other government regulations; he talked about handling personnel problems and jobsite injuries; he related every detail he could think of that was part of his typical day.

At no time in this presentation did the member mention the organization. He wasn't asked to make any connection between his daily challenges and his membership in the organization. He answered a few questions and then left. The important part of the program then began.

After the member left, the organization's staff director asked each staff person to list all of the times his/her department could have helped the member during the member's typical day. The staff then went around and told what they had listed, and they came up with a combined list of several ways the organization could have made an impact on the member's day. It was a great way to get some empathy for the challenges their typical members faced each day, and it also made the staff more aware of the value of membership.

c) As new members join the organization, go to their websites or the website of the company, organization, or institution for whom they work. These web sites allow organizations to learn about the new members' priorities, how they market their products or services, what their corporate or organizational culture is, who their key leaders are, etc. Having this information will help the organization gain a greater understanding of why these members joined – *for the empathy!*

Rule Number 8
Never Underestimate the WOW Factor

While sitting at my desk during a typical work day, I realized that my wife's birthday was coming up and, as usual, I had waited until the last minute to decide what to get her. Over the (30-plus) years of marriage, I had been pretty good about buying thoughtful gifts, but I was really running out of ideas. I knew she appreciated anything I got her, but this year I really wanted to do something – anything - a little different. When I went to check my email that day, a pop-up ad appeared for an online greeting card service. I thought, well, I've always bought a card along with her gift, but maybe this little electronic card would seem more creative.

I had never purchased an online card before, so I clicked on the web site, and started navigating through the system. I first was instructed to select an occasion - that was easy enough to do. Then, I had to choose from among the dozens of birthday card designs (there were probably hundreds more choices but I was overwhelmed after a few pages of them). Next I had to put in the name of the person to whom I was sending the card, as well as entering my own name.

Finally, I was given a blank space where I could write in any message I wanted or I could choose from among the messages the service provided. Being a somewhat creative person, I wrote my own message.

The last steps included reading the entire card again, approving everything by checking a box, and then entering my payment information (credit card number, etc.). Finally, I clicked the box that said "I'm ready to send my greeting."

After clicking the "send" button, I almost instantaneously heard my computer say "You've got mail!"

I checked my email account and saw that I had a message from the greeting card company. I clicked it on and it said, "Mark - Your birthday message has been sent to Barbara."

Not a form letter thanking me for purchasing from them, not a generic "Your mail has been sent," but an immediate, personalized reassurance that my transaction had been successful.

Do you know what I said to myself ?

I said, "WOW! That's really great. I just sent this card a couple of seconds ago, and they have already sent me a personal message to let me know not to worry, that everything is okay. WOW!"

About two hours later, I again heard the familiar, "You've got mail." I went to my email and saw that there was another message from the greeting card company. My first thought was that this was going to be an official confirmation that my credit card had gone through, or maybe the opposite, that it didn't get through. Then I started thinking that maybe they were contacting me to try to sell me some other service or product.

When I opened the email, it simply said "Mark – Just wanted you to know that Barbara has collected the birthday card you sent."

And I said to myself, "WOW! Is that neat, or what? Not only do they reassure me that my message was sent, they assure me it was also received and opened, and they do it using my name, and hers. WOW!"

After an experience like this, the chances are pretty good that I'll do business with this company again.

Membership organizations can learn a lesson from this incident - *never underestimate the "WOW Factor."*

There are many times throughout the year when organizations have a chance to really WOW their members. Unfortunately, organizations don't always realize the opportunities are there, and they let them slip by. In order to WOW members, organizations should be aware of these opportunities, or they have to create them.

Here are some suggestions for doing both.

1) Start tracking phone calls, emails, fax requests, etc. to develop a list of most frequently asked questions. Don't just make up a list of what the organization's leaders <u>think</u> members/customers are most interested in, get some real data. Use this information to create the frequently asked questions list.

2) Use the frequently asked questions list to reposition the pages on the organization's website. Be sure members can get to these questions (and answers) with no more than three clicks of the computer mouse.

3) Keep track of problems and complaints from members/customers. Use this list to determine if there is a need to hold more customer/member service training sessions or a need to change some of the organization's policies and procedures.

4) Be sure to add the organization's member/customer service policies to the information on its website. Let members/customers know what to expect - and then exceed their expectations!

5) Acknowledge everything, even the most basic communications. Reassure members/customers that their messages are getting through.

6) Cross-train all staffers in every aspect of member/customer service. Give every staffer the tools needed to deal with member requests.

7) Ask each staff member to spend just a few hours serving as the organization's receptionist. This will greatly increase their understanding of what is important to members/customers (and will probably assure that staffers will have a much greater appreciation for the receptionist).

8) Make sure that all staffers have access to the organization's membership database, so that while they talk to a member they can see how active the member is, what the member's interests are, etc.

9) Automate personal messages that go to members at designated times, messages such as birthday wishes or congratulations on membership anniversaries.

10) When a member contacts the organization with a complaint, have a well-communicated method of dealing with problems and following up. Address the complaint as quickly as possible, and write down any commitments or promises made to the member. Track the member's complaint (if it is being taken care of by others) and make sure the problem is completely resolved. Then close the loop by contacting the member to be sure the member is satisfied with the solution.

11) Be sure the organization's website address is on the organization's after-hours answering message.

Rule Number 9
Learn to Compete With the Big Boys

One of the points of emphasis in this book has been the concept that the private sector has become one of the toughest competitors for membership organizations. In addition to competition from internet service providers, nonprofits are also in competition with many private businesses, large and small, who now claim to be able to provide products and services that were once the purview of membership organizations.

It would be easy to look at this competition and believe that there is no way that nonprofits can match these private companies. These firms have such huge resources that nonprofits can't reasonably be expected to compete at the highest levels.

Maybe there's another way of looking at it. Maybe what membership organizations need to do is spend less time complaining about these competitors and more time learning from them.

If these companies are so good at customer service and keeping customers, maybe membership organizations should learn from their success. Instead of fighting the competition, maybe membership organizations should be emulating the competition. Not-for-profit is a designation given to membership organizations by some government agency, it doesn't have to be a business philosophy. Remember - even nonprofits can - and should - be run in a businesslike manner. They are just different kinds of businesses.

Here are some techniques and policies that three of the world's most successful corporations use to enhance customer service and create repeat customers. Many of the techniques they use have parallels in the nonprofit world.

BellSouth

When you are one of the largest telephone and communications companies in the United States, with millions and millions of customers, maintaining a high level of customer service is an extremely difficult task. Of course, no company can expect to make 100% of its customers happy all the time, but BellSouth has earned a reputation for being one of the leaders in its field. In fact, the company has won award after award for its customer service methods. In an interview after receiving one these awards, the Chairman of BellSouth was asked if he felt that customer service, in general, is better than it was in the past. His reply wasn't really surprising.

"It's not really just a question of better or worse," he said, "it's just that expectations are higher. Convenience is more important. But it's still about treating customers with courtesy and respect, and about listening to them and trying to understand their needs and how to satisfy their needs."

Here are some of the philosophies and techniques that have made BellSouth a leader in customer service.

-A Commitment to Care.

BellSouth believes that good customer service has to be part of a corporate culture, not just a slogan. The company understands that every employee plays a part in good customer service, regardless of his or her position in the company.

Nonprofits can institutionalize a customer/member service culture, too. The first step is to develop some member service policies and standards. This can't be just a reminder to the staff to answer the phone quickly and be polite. Real commitment means identifying as many ways as possible to actually measure good customer service, and then setting standards of good performance. Try to identify what top-level performance means in areas like turnaround time on orders; how many times a phone rings before it's answered; how many times a caller gets transferred before speaking to the right person; how accurate the member listings are in the organization's database and directory; etc.

-Continuous Improvement

BellSouth believes that no company ever stays at the top of its field by being satisfied with its past perform-ance. The company is constantly reviewing all of the customer service information it can gather and discussing ways to improve.

Nonprofits don't often have the luxury of high-cost customer service surveys and outside marketing consultants. They have to rely more on internal sources of information to determine how they're doing and where can they can improve. This means that nonprofits need to set up a system to get constant input from their staff and volunteer leaders. This input needs to be more than just a weekly or monthly meeting to ask people how they "feel" about the organization's performance. There needs to be a specific set of guidelines established for what is being measured and what the organization is doing to make continuous progress toward better member service and higher retention.

-Top-down Involvement

BellSouth's Chairman admitted that the company's top executives are not in touch with customers often enough. When they do interact with customers it's a big deal – to the customer. The Chairman believes it should be a big deal to the executives as well.

Nonprofits need the same type of leadership philosophy, only more so. If the top leaders in the organization (Board members, officers, top-level staff) aren't committed to better member service through a systematic approach, then the other staff and members are unlikely to be as concerned about it as they should be. The organization's Board of Directors and top staff need to adopt a formal, specific, written set of customer service policies and guidelines. These need to be developed with input from various sources, and then communicated to everyone in the organization's staff and volunteer leadership. These policies should be reviewed frequently and used as part of the evaluation of the organization's retention efforts.

-Ownership of a Problem

BellSouth has a very interesting philosophy regarding who is responsible for solving their customers' problems. According to their Chairman, "No matter who you are, when you come in contact with a customer who has a problem, you own that problem until you help the customer get it solved."

Nonprofits need to take note of this concept. If there was ever a great slogan for member service and member retention, it is "You own the problem until it is solved." That doesn't mean that the leader or staffer who is the first contact with the member and his/her problem has to be the person with the answer to the problem. It's very possible that the member's problem is better handled by another staff person or volunteer leader. It DOES mean that the person who first interacted with the member is responsible not just for transferring the problem to someone else, but also for making sure that the problem is solved.

It also means that everyone on the membership organization's staff needs to buy into the concept of top-level member service. It means that the days of "It's not my job" are over. It means that staffers can no longer consider themselves or their departments separate entities, dedicated to only one area such as legislation or education. It means that all leaders, volunteer and staff, have to be willing to accept "reminders" and inquiries from others who have asked them to help solve a member problem. It means that the organization's leadership needs to establish a teambuilding system that will create a culture that focuses not on the organization, but on the members.

-Employee empowerment

BellSouth's management knows that the concept of "owning a problem" can only be effective if the people who are asked to take ownership of a problem also have the authority to solve the problem. BellSouth empowers its employees to make as many decisions as possible in the area of customer service. In BellSouth's world, there is a basic understanding that customers don't want to explain their problem to a person only to find out that the person has to ask a supervisor or other employee for permission or authority to solve the problem.

Because the majority of **nonprofits** usually don't have millions of members/customers and hundreds of designated customer service staffers, this notion of employee empowerment becomes even more critical. It must be extremely frustrating for a member to contact an organization with only a few staffers and be told "You'll have to wait until the Exec gets back. He's the only one who can authorize that."

This doesn't imply that every staffer should be able to do everything necessary to meet a customer's needs. Sometimes there are financial or legal considerations, sometimes the member's request is outside the scope of the organization's policies, etc. Most of the time, however, member requests will fall into a few general areas. In these areas, staffers should be given as much information and discretion as possible. For this to happen, the organization's top staffers must be willing and able to delegate effectively, to cross-train more employees, and to build a culture of mutual support within the organization.

classmates.com

Classmates.com is one of the few internet companies that has truly touched a "hot button" with its customer base. It's somewhat unique in the private sector because it refers to its customers as "members." That's because *classmates.com* is really nothing more than a large, universal alumni association. The concept of the website is to help graduates of high schools and colleges stay in touch with their classmates - *forever*!

To say that they have touched a hot button is really a huge understatement. Although the company is only a few years old, they have (as of the time this book is being written) over 37 million "members." Not all of these members are actually dues paying members, because *classmates.com* allows people to register without becoming full members (they know that the more people they have in their system, the better chance they have to put people in touch with others). Once these people are in the system, however, the company has captured their contact information and can afford to gradually entice the nonpaying members to upgrade to full member status.

Classmates.com also knows that advertisers are pretty impressed by any organization that has the ability to communicate with 37 million people instantaneously. The success of the website has spawned spin-off businesses, such as a television show and other marketing operations.

Let's look at some of the things that make *classmates.com* a success and see if nonprofits can adapt these techniques.

-Technology engagement

Classmates.com is completely technology-based. In the words of one of their members, "There is no 'there' there." *Classmates.com* is not a physical place, it is a virtual place. You can get "involved" only electronically - access the site, look for classmates, correspond by email. If you don't think this doesn't sound like much of a reunion, think again. People are in constant contact and conversation on their sites, reliving their past and enjoying finding out where people are and what they are doing.

And here's one of the most interesting aspects of *classmates.com*. Guess who is (or most certainly will be) most comfortable in this virtual alumni association? The Millennials! The very demographic segment that most organizations can't seem to attract and retain (see Chapter 6).

Nonprofits have some great opportunities in looking at what *classmates.com* has done and making some inroads with their members, especially the younger ones. In order to get more of the newer/younger members engaged, nonprofits need to provide as wide a range of technology options as possible. The more ways members can get information, gain knowledge, contact their peers, join or renew, purchase products and services, and engage in some level of organizational activity, the better chance there will be that they will come back again next year.

-Cross-selling products and services

Classmates.com does an excellent job of cross-selling its products and services. When you contact the site for any reason, there will invariably be an "invitation" to take advantage of other aspects of the site. For example, if you request information on a reunion, the site might ask if you'd be interested in helping organize one.

This is similar to what *amazon.com* does when a person orders books through its online bookstore. Just before clicking the button to complete the purchase of a book from *amazon.com,* there is a little note that says "People reading this book are also reading....", and they mention other books in the same genre or by the same author. All the customer needs to do is click the book title to be taken to the listing for that book. *Amazon.com* sells millions of additional books this way.

Nonprofits need to pick up on this technique - NOW. For example, when a member orders a publication online, the organization's website should send an automatic acknowledgement thanking the member for the order and then saying something such as "We're having a seminar on the same topic that is covered in the publication you just ordered. To find out more about the seminar, click here." Take advantage of every member contact to find at least one more way to get the member engaged.

(For more ideas on this type of member engagement, see Rule Number 10)

-**Personalization**

Classmates.com personalizes almost everything. It doesn't say "Dear member" anywhere. It calls its members by name, and sends a personalized message ("Mark-three more classmates from your year have joined *classmates.com*. Click here to see who they are and catch up with what they're doing.") People love to see their name in print, and seeing it on a website is just as good. What's even better, it shows that the organization cares about the individual, not just "fellow members."

Nonprofits need to wake up to the fact that "Dear Fellow Member" is no longer an acceptable way to communicate with members. In addition to being impersonal, it is somewhat of an insult to members because they know that the technology exists to personalize everything.

Marriott Corporation

The Marriott Corporation is a company that has built a reputation based not just on customer service, but on the overriding concept of quality control. From its beginning as an A & W Root Beer stand in Washington, D.C. in the 1920's to the huge multinational business it is today, Marriott has instituted a corporate culture of setting quality standards for everything and then managing the company in order to live up to those standards.

-Empathy training

Marriott works hard to instill the notion of quality control in all of its employees (not just the service people). One of the techniques they employ is something that, for lack of a better term, is known as "empathy training." Every management-level employee is asked to go out into Marriott's various business enterprises (hotels, food service, etc.) and perform the work required of the people who are employed in the areas for which the manager is responsible. This means that every manager is going to experience (at least for a short while) the challenges, frustrations, and rewards of working for Marriott in these various jobs.

For example, when the new division head took over Marriott's Fast Food Division years ago, he spent time working in what was then Marriott-owned Roy Rogers restaurants and carry-out stores. He helped prepare the food, serve it, and clean up after the store had closed. While he didn't actually spend years working in the fast food outlets, he spent enough time to get a feel for what his employees faced, and what his customers experienced in Marriott-owned restaurants. He not only could understand what customers wanted and expected, he knew what employees needed to do to meet those expectations.

Nonprofit membership organizations can use the same technique to give staffers at least a small idea of what members face every day in their jobs and in their professions. One association asked its staffers to spend a day with one of the organization's members. Association staff members actually went out and spent an entire day with a member, from the opening of the business in the morning to the last after-hours meeting in the evening. The idea was to let the staffers really get some insight into the problems members faced. The goal was simple - when the staffer picked up the phone and listened to the requests of members calling their Headquarters office, the staff could actually "picture" the situation the member was describing.

By looking at these successful companies, membership organizations can pick up many ideas for enhanced member/customer service, and retention. Here are some additional tips on giving the best member service.

1. *Ask the right questions.*
Sometimes members aren't really sure what they want from an organization. Even when asked something as simple as "How may we help you?" there can be a miscommunication. Members actually don't know how the organization can help them unless they know everything that the organization does. What they *do* know, in all cases, is what problem they need solved. Try to guide them into explaining what their problem is, and get them in touch with the correct person or department.

2. *Give members options where possible, but don't overwhelm them.*

Yes, staffers want to be as helpful as possible, and they want to offer members options on pricing, delivery, payment, etc., but be careful about giving members too many options. Usually the member wants the problem solved or question answered as quickly and easily as possible. This is one of the reasons people get frustrated with phone menus that keep asking them to make selection after selection before the system allows the member to talk to someone who can answer the question.

3. *Learn to be a little "bilingual".*

Sometimes people who work for membership organizations forget that the members and customers contacting the organization aren't familiar with everything the organization does. Staffers can fall into the trap of using names and initials and references that are well-known to staff and organizational leaders but not necessarily to members at large. Be careful to speak the "language" of members/customers.

4. *Repeat important information.*

When a member request requires some sort of follow-up action by a staff person, be sure to repeat important information before breaking off the contact with the member. Reconfirm what is to be done, in what time frame, etc. so there are no misconceptions about what is going to be done. If staffers make sure they are clear on what members' expectations are, they have a good chance of meeting or exceeding them.

5. *Set quality control standards on everything the organization does.*
Membership organizations need to emulate the "big boys" by establishing standards of performance on all aspects of customer service. Tracking the organization's performance in such things as turn around time on orders, meeting deadlines on publications, returning phone calls in a specified time frame, etc., isn't supposed to put undo pressure on overworked staff members. It is supposed to remind everyone of the organization's commitment to meeting member/customer needs.

6. *When in doubt about whether or not the organization can "do it" for a member, DO IT! Handle the internal battles later.*
Membership organizations must empower their staffers to make good, common sense judgments when handling member requests. Within reason (i.e. within the legal and financial guidelines of their organization), staffers should be encouraged to give members what they want as often as possible. Staffers should handle the "internal" battles after the member's problem has been solved.

7. *Understand that responsiveness is probably the number one evaluator of good member service.*

The most important trait of good member service is the most obvious - responsiveness. This refers to how fast a member request for information or a product is fulfilled. It also refers to how responsive the staff member was when dealing with the member/customer. Was the staffer's attitude positive? Did the staffer make the member/customer feel as though the request for assistance was somehow interrupting something more important? It's the overall experience the member has on each transaction that will determine if the member feels that the organization is responsive. Fortunately, responsiveness is also measurable, so standards can be set for good response.

8. *Handle problems as they arise.*
If a problem looks as though it might grow into something worse, don't take the attitude of "We'll cross that bridge when we come to it." Stop and find ways to correct the problem immediately. This philosophy of finding solutions to problems as they arise has saved private companies millions of dollars over the years. They found that to delay dealing with current problems only creates more expensive problems later on.

9. *Don't panic if something goes wrong.*
Improving an organization's member/customer service is an important goal, but the effort must focus on continuous improvement, not on perfection. No organization is ever going to be perfect in member/customer service. If something goes wrong (and it will), the ability to retain that member or

customer is dependent upon how your organization handles the situation. Customer service surveys over the years indicate that a vast majority of members/customers who have a problem with an organization's products or services *will* do business with that organization again, as long as the problem is solved to the member/customer's satisfaction. Apologize for mistakes, ask the member/customer what it will take to make the situation right, and then (within reason) do what they ask.

How To Measure "Good" Member Service

Every organization wants to improve member service (and retention) but sometimes it's hard to determine what real improvement means. It's imperative for organizations striving for better member service to measure their progress. Here is a list of items various organizations measure in order to monitor their success in the area of member service.

Number of calls per day & per month
Year to year comparison of calls by month
Average wait time per call
Calls received per hour
Number of call transfers
Average length of calls
Number & type of complaints received

Total number of members per month by category (vs. previous years, etc.)
Total number of new members per month by category

Total renewals per month by category
Response rate to renewal notices (1st, 2nd, 3rd, etc.)
Sources of new members
Number of website visits
Number of website visits by category
Website pages most frequently visited
Website pages by length of visit
Most frequently asked questions by phone inquiries
Most frequently asked questions via email or web visitors
Attendance at meetings (by category of member)
Attendance at educational programs (by category of member)

Attendee evaluations
% of member participants, total
% of member participants by event/function
% of member participants by membership category

Bad address email returns
Bad address mailing returns

On time publication of various publications (electronic and printed)
Number of typographical and grammatical errors per communication
Survey results
Performance vs. same period previous years (trend)

Rule Number 10
Technology Rules

When the dot-com boom collapsed in the 1990's and a huge number of internet companies went broke, a lot of people were thinking, "Good. They were never REAL companies anyway. They just created a lot of wealth for some computer geeks and took a bunch of venture capital down the tubes." Others were probably thinking, "I told you so. This ecommerce thing was just a fad. People still want to do business with real, live people and companies, not a bunch of computers. I'm glad our organization didn't fall into the trap of getting into a bunch of expensive 'portals' and 'hyperlinks'."

As much as some people would like to think that a lot of this technical jargon and electronic communication is going to go away, and that life will return to "normal," that isn't going to happen. What people were experiencing was just the normal shake-out of any new industry or technology. (Don't forget that in the 1920's and 1930's there were dozens of companies manufacturing automobiles.) Like it or not, it will be necessary to deal with this technology revolution from now on. This is truly a "revolution" not because technological changes are new, but because it is so hard to deal with the *speed* at which technologies change.

The impact of technology has been discussed in numerous places in this book, usually in the context of how technological advances have created challenges for membership organizations. However, technology is a double-edged sword in membership retention programs. While it does create an environment of raised expectations, it also creates opportunities for organizations to engage and retain members.

Before determining how to use technology in member retention, each organization must first be sure it is doing everything possible to create a positive membership environment. This means not only having an effective value message for members and prospects, but also delivering that message effectively. A great message means nothing if it doesn't get to the right people the right way. Just because an organization has something of value to offer members and potential members doesn't mean these people are out there trying to find the organization – the organization needs to *find them*, and then convince them of the value of membership.

Sometimes organizational leaders (staff and volunteer) get too close to the organization's information, and they don't interpret the information the way members and prospects will. Organizations need to constantly search for the one message that will help the organization *stand out* from all the others. Given the incredible amount of competition organizations have for the attention of members and prospects, there is a tremendous need to work on developing the clearest possible message and delivering it with the utmost efficiency.

Staying "On Message"

It has always been a struggle for membership marketers to decide what to put into their membership message. They hate to leave out any of the really great benefits their organization offers, but at the same time they don't want the message to get too cluttered with a long list of programs and services. This decision on what to include and what to leave out has become even more problematic in today's electronic communications era. It is hard enough to get members to read short email messages. Trying to get them to absorb a list of membership benefits is an even tougher challenge. The key is to focus the message on the needs of the member, without making it so narrow that the organization loses the chance to entice some marginally interested people or companies.

One way to determine what the organization's core value message should be is to use a tried and true marketing test known as the "need-to-know, nice-to-know" theory. Figure out what members *need* to know in order to make a decision to rejoin, or to respond, or to attend, or to go to your website, or whatever decision you want them to make. Use this "need-to-know" information to get their attention and get them started toward the action you want. Then, if there is room in the letter or brochure or email, identify some of the information that would be "nice-to-know" about the organization or the event. Although this technique for determining content has been around for a long time, it still has some validity today. In fact, given the ultra-short attention span of most members/prospects, maybe it's a good time to start using this technique again.

Spanning the Spam

Of course, just having the right message doesn't assure it will get through to the intended target. Organizations are facing a critical challenge in communications. In order to get value messages out as fast as possible (a true necessity in today's business world), organizations rely on electronic communications. However, even though most people are getting comfortable with electronic communications (studies show that email has overtaken the telephone as the number one form of business communication in the United States) there are still four things causing havoc in the battle to get members' attention and loyalty. These four things are related. They are:

1) spam
2) spam filters
3) viruses
4) "do not contact" regulations

Spam (junk email) is causing problems in two ways. First, it clutters up so much of the members'/prospects' email that legitimate messages are getting lost. If members don't recognize who sent the email, there is little chance it will get opened. Even if an organization can get members to open emails, the organization has only a short period of time (actually, about 2.5 seconds, according to the Direct Marketing Association) to get members' attention and to get them to read further. This clutter causes people to delete many daily email messages, and the level of frustration with these intrusions rises to the point that people are already upset and time-challenged by the time they get around to reading these membership messages.

Spam filters are designed to help keep some of that clutter off people's computer screens, but not all spam filters operate the same way. Many messages are getting caught in spam filters, messages that members probably wanted and needed. Because the computer doesn't recognize the content, or the sender, or the way some of the messages are formatted, they are sent through the spam filter. Knowing that the filter picks up some wanted messages, people then have to review all the spam anyway, just to make sure that nothing they wanted got caught. Where's the time and effort savings here?

In addition to all the spam, people have to deal with the literal *plague* of computer **viruses** that have infected millions of computers. The fear of viruses invading their computers may cause members and prospects to delete anything that has an attachment, or is sent from an unrecognized source, or that is forwarded from an unknown source. Some companies configure their computers to prevent the downloading of attachments that don't meet certain criteria.

This could mean the organization's value message is among those messages being automatically rejected. It might mean members and prospects never see the message, however on target and effective it might be. If organizations can't get members to open and read these messages, how will they ever get them to join or participate?

As if that wasn't enough, now associations and other membership organizations are getting caught in the middle of the **"Do not contact"** issue. The "do not call" list started it, then came the "Do not fax" ruling, and now the "Do not email" movement has moved in. While the not-for-profit community has sought relief from some of these new laws, it just seems as though the battle for the time and attention of members and prospects gets tougher every day.

So what's the answer? Maybe there isn't any one answer, but there are a few things organizations can do to help get their messages through to the target markets. Here are some suggestions on ways to send electronic messages that will actually be read (once they get through the spam filters) and will receive the attention and response needed from members and customers.

-Develop attachment-free communications systems. Just because it's easy for organization staffers to attach a memo and send it with the email doesn't mean anyone is reading it. There are too many auto-deletes of attachments because of virus fears.

-Develop and communicate unique signatures on your email communications to your members. Give members the information they need to help their system recognize and accept your organization's messages.

-Automate responses to the most common communications and guide members/prospects to appropriate web pages and sites.

-Alert members to the various addresses that will be coming from the organization and get members to set their computer systems up to let these messages through.

-Don't use capital letters in emails. It makes it look as though the sender is SHOUTING!

-Try to cover just one topic in an email. If a response is needed to more than one topic, number the items so there is no confusion over which answer goes to which question.

-To avoid "email tag," and the inconvenience of opening email responses such as "okay" or "fine," indicate clearly in your email if a return reply is necessary.

-Be careful about quality. Remember that the image of the organization is "attached" to every piece of correspondence. Set standards for emails being sent from the organization to its members. This is an area that can be monitored and improved upon.

-Think about whether or not email is really the right format for each message. When making a formal request or sending a contract, maybe the written word (written on paper, that is) is a more appropriate way to communicate.

-Try to anticipate any questions an outgoing email might raise and cover these anticipated questions in the message. Alleviate the necessity of the receiver sending an email back just to ask a question that could have been anticipated.

-Be extremely careful when responding to questions generated via some sort of list or group. First, there is the obvious threat of a virus being sent to computers through the messages received from others. Second, if the sender has sent copies to others, those people will get all the replies, too.

-Make everything readable. Don't make the type size too small for people to read easily and quickly.

-Unless it is absolutely necessary to getting the message across effectively, avoid using color in email copy. It may help make the message look fancy on the screen, but when the recipient goes to print the message it may be on a non-color printer. In these cases the color copy will look faded. Remember, too, that even if the receiver has a color printer, he/she doesn't necessarily want to waste expensive color ink on routine messages.

-Spellcheck, spellcheck, spellcheck. This is another aspect of quality control that can be measured. Just because email is fast doesn't mean it has to be sloppy.

-Do not send confidential information in an email without being 100% positive that it is going to be received only by the intended recipient.

-Make it easy for the receiver to contact the sender in the format that is most comfortable for the receiver. Make sure messages contain a signature line that includes all of the various ways to contact the sender (phone, fax. email, website, etc.)

-Use the "Out of the Office" message to let members know that it might be a while before their messages will be returned.

Using technology for member communications, engagement, involvement, and retention isn't an option any more, it's a necessity. Technology will continue to change the world in which members and their organizations exist, and membership organizations who make technology a tool, rather than a barrier, will be the organizations that prosper in the new membership marketplace.

Rule Number 11
Take the Mystery Out of Membership

Several years ago, in a presentation to a group of nonprofit executives, Bill Marriott, Chairman of the Marriott Corporation (see Chapter 9), told how his company's famous quality control culture and attention to detail was institutionalized by his father, J. Willard Marriott, the company's founder.

"My Dad believed that you had to be out among your customers to really know what they wanted," he said. "He would go into one of his Hot Shoppes (the name of Marriott's first chain of restaurants, which became famous as the "place to be" for generations of teenagers in the Washington, D.C. area) and just be a customer. He wouldn't tell the manager who he was, but he would talk to as many customers as possible. This was long before anyone ever heard of focus groups. He felt that the best way to get customers to come back was to give them what they wanted, and to do that you had to have the same experience in the restaurant as they did."

"To show you how much of a detail man he was when it came to customer service," Marriott continued, "he would listen to every customer comment, test it to see if it was a true customer concern, and correct it if it was warranted. One customer complained that the bacon we served was too chewy, so Dad tasted it and agreed.

We started serving crispier bacon. Customers told us they could tell the difference and they liked it. Years later, on the day my Dad died, I was at his house when he sat down in his favorite chair, and his last words were 'Make sure the bacon is crisp.'"

J. Willard Marriott left behind a customer service and quality control system that came to be known in the Marriott Corporation as "Management by Walking Around". His theory was that no Marriott manager could possibly find out what was going on in the company while sitting in an office behind a desk. This was true whether the manager was a Roy Rogers fast food store manager, a Marriott hotel manager, or the vice president of the entire corporation (or even the Chairman of the Board, for that matter). He instituted a policy of having every Marriott senior executive spend several days a week out of the office, visiting Marriott properties and outlets. This philosophy probably started in the early days of his company, when he and his wife used to stand for hours at various intersections in the Washington, D.C. area to determine if the vehicle and pedestrian traffic made these locations good potential spots for their next Hot Shoppe.

Bill Marriott gave another example of how this technique worked. He said that when he visits his company's flagship hotel in Washington, D.C. he tries as often as possible to enter through the main entrance and use the escalators and elevators used by the public, rather than entering through the private/staff entrances because he wants to see what is going on. One day when he was going up in the public elevator to a management meeting, a pizza delivery person got on the elevator with him, carrying several large pizzas, and pushed the button for the 6th floor. Marriott asked, "Where are you going with those?" and the delivery person said, "I've got one on the 6th floor, and two on the 8th floor." Marriott then said, "Do you deliver a lot of pizzas here?" and the delivery person replied, "Oh, yeah. We're here all the time."

This was more than Marriott could take. Here he was, in the top property of the Marriott Corporation, a company founded on food service, and customers were ordering food *in* from outside the hotel. Within a matter of just a few short weeks Marriotts across the U.S., and eventually in other countries, started offering pizza on their menus. If Bill Marriott had taken the private entrance and used the private elevators, this change may never have taken place.

Management by Walking Around proved to be a highly successful management philosophy and customer service/quality control technique for Marriott. It is also an excellent technique and philosophy for membership organizations.

In today's marketplace, many organizations already use a similar technique but they don't know it as Management by Walking Around. Today this practice is known as **Mystery Shopping**. It's the same basic principal with a different name. Mystery Shopping in a membership organization is an excellent (maybe the BEST) way to really get to experience the organization the way members do.

To effectively use Mystery Shopping in member service and member retention efforts, organizations have to move away from looking at things from the viewpoint of their staff and leaders, and actually look at things from the perspective of someone who isn't in any way involved in running the organization. It isn't just finding out how fast the mail gets out, or how long it takes to receive a publication that was ordered, that makes Mystery Shopping a powerful tool for membership retention. It's also the ability to see, from a completely objective view, what type of member service *culture* the organization has.

There are two basic ways to use mystery shopping in the search for higher retention. One is to have a staffer or leader do the mystery shopping. The other is to have someone completely outside the organization do the mystery shopping.

Having a staffer or leader do the mystery shopping can be productive because these people know what questions to ask, what areas to probe, and what aspects of the organization are the most vulnerable to less than desired member service performance. It allows the organization to focus on the areas of greatest concern and pinpoint the places that need the most time and resources.

Having an outsider serve as the Mystery Shopper opens up a whole new world of opportunities for improving member service and retention. Because the Mystery Shopper has absolutely no expectations or preconceived ideas about what will happen, or even what *good* member/customer service is supposed to look like, there will be a fresh view of every interaction with the organization. From filling out and sending in the application, to receiving the new member information, to trying to participate in some way, to going through the renewal process, this completely open perspective can be invaluable in the search for higher retention.

There are many ways to use mystery shopping in your membership retention efforts. For example, mystery shopping can be used to:

1) *Evaluate member/customer service effectiveness*
Have a Mystery Shopper join the organization. Ask the person to keep track of all of the contacts made by the organization, making appropriate notes about responsiveness, courtesy, etc. Things that should be monitored are:
> -speed of contact after the member joins
> (measure lag time)
> -format of follow up (email, written, more than
> one format, etc.)

-frequency of contact from the organization, especially in the first few months
-speed of fulfilling orders (acknowledgement and receipt of order)
-effectiveness of communications (readable, interesting, etc.)

2) *Evaluate administrative functions*
Sometimes it's the simple things that most impress members. A Mystery Shopper can identify administrative functions that should be improved, too.
-Is all information regarding the Mystery Shopper accurate and up-to-date?
-Do mailings look clean, with labels on straight and neat?
-Are changes handled quickly and accurately?

3) *Evaluate the organization's staff*
This is a very sensitive area. The organization's staffers are probably not going to be happy when they find out they are being "tested" by a mystery shopper. This should be handled very carefully. Staffers must understand that it isn't a question of being spied upon, it's a question of what can be done to improve member service and retention. The Mystery Shopper can give some insight into:
-How quickly phone calls are answered
-How many times callers are transferred from one person to another
-Whether or not the person answering the phone is courteous and helpful

-Whether or not the receptionist is knowledgeable about where or to whom the caller should be transferred
-What level of integrity the staff has (do the staff members make inappropriate comments about other staffers or volunteer leaders)
-How aware the staff is of organizational policies, and how consistent they are in enforcing them
-Whether or not the staff is empowered to solve member problems vs. having to seek authority from someone else

4) *Evaluate the organization's communications efforts*
Part of the frustration many organizations find in dealing with members is that answers to many of the inquiries members make have already been sent to them in various communications from the organization. Mystery shopping can help the organization:

1) Find out how quickly information is getting to members
2) Find out whether or not the messages are getting through clearly
3) Find out how accurate the organization's records are
4) Find out how effective the staff's writing skills are
5) Find out what format is most effective for getting information to members

For the mystery shopper method of evaluation to be as effective as possible, the Mystery Shopper should:

1) Join the organization.
2) Register for all functions - educational programs, conferences, webcasts, online learning, etc.
3) Subscribe to all organizational publications
4) Call the organization office at least once a month to ask for information on varying products, services, events, etc.
5) Visit the organization's web site weekly to see what is updated and to get basic information about the organization's programs and services
6) Order publications or products in various ways- online, via mail, via fax, on the phone
7) Fill out and return all surveys
8) At renewal time, DON'T renew. Keep track of all renewal-related contacts and communications
9) Volunteer for a committee position or appointment

By participating in as many activities as possible, the Mystery Shopper will be able to get an overview of the level of service the organization can provide, and can evaluate the organization's current member service capabilities. Rather than giving the organization *opinions* about good or bad service (always a difficult thing to do, since "good service" means different things to different people), the Mystery Shopper should be focused on reporting the facts. If the organization has established reasonable measurement criteria for member service, the information from the Mystery

Shopper(s) can be used in a more credible evaluation of performance. This also provides guidance on other member/customer service factors that should be measured and evaluated.

Whether it is called Mystery Shopping or Management by Walking Around, getting an outsider's perspective on the level of member/customer service the organization offers can be of great help in the ongoing effort to improve value for members and strengthen their commitment to the organization. By using this technique effectively, organizations can discover keys to providing the best possible membership experience and, as a result, increase retention.

Rule Number 12
Virtual Value Still Equals Value

Every organization is coping with the challenges of attracting and involving more members in an ever-changing marketplace. Organizations should **stop** dealing with these changes by using the same methods of member communication that they have always used, and begin doing the things that will actually work with these current – and succeeding – generations of members and prospects. Organizations need to be flexible, and they need to be realistic.

First, organizations have to understand that things such as newsletters, Friday faxes, town meetings at conventions, etc., are techniques that will work with the people they are already working with, not with the new generations of members.

Second, if organizations think that their members are going to show up in the same numbers as they have in the past, they need to think again. In the era of the 24-hour work day, organizational meetings are falling lower and lower on members' priority lists. Let's see – members have three choices each day after their normal work day. They can spend some quality time with their family; they can sit down at their home computer and get a two hour head start on that project or report that's due; or they can go to a meeting of their trade or professional association, or some other nonprofit organization.

Care to guess who loses?

Third, instead of wringing their hands and wondering what to do, organizations need to get with the program. If members want options on how they can participate, give it to them.

In previous eras, organizations considered their "good" members to be those who were involved in leadership roles at the national or affiliate level. Of course, those people are still good members. But in today's world people can't be counted on to get involved like that. Organizations need to consider a new and innovative alternative - virtual membership.

Why not just create a *category* called Virtual Member? Let members sign up to get whatever they want from the organization through electronic communication. They don't want a monthly magazine or a bi-weekly newsletter. Let them read whatever they want to read online. They don't need a publications catalogue - they'll get that off the web site. If they decide to attend a conference, they'll pay a premium (less than non-members, more than full members). Affiliate or chapter membership? Make it optional. Do they want help from a staff specialist on a particular issue? Give them a special email address. Do they want access to special interest groups or technical divisions? No problem. Add a small fee to the Virtual Membership fee (full members get it included in their annual dues). Time for renewal? They have to renew online, of course, with special incentives to upgrade to full membership, and to renew early.

Okay, doubters, let's hear it. "We'll lose advertising revenue for our publications." "We'll have fewer people attending our meetings." "Full members will feel that these people are getting membership cheaper than they are. Why shouldn't everyone support the organization equally?"

Guess what? Most members weren't coming to the meetings anyway. Many members aren't reading the publications, and, in fact, they may actually resent having their mailboxes full of things they don't want. They DO support the organization – they just want to do it in their own way.

Flexibility is going to be the key to survival in this new marketplace. Until everyone is on the same level in terms of communications technology, organizations must be able to meet the needs of all types of members.

Virtual membership shouldn't be a slogan or a gimmick – it should be an option.

Here are 10 things organizations can do to make sure that even those members who don't show up will perceive value in membership in their organization.

1) *Make the organization's website as user-friendly as possible*

The web sites of many volunteer membership organizations are difficult to navigate. The home page is bursting with all of the latest organization news, and there is a list of departments on the left side of the page. That's fine, but the home page really should be a starting point for problem solving, not just a gateway to the rest of the site.

Research on web site usage reveals some interesting information. For example, according to one internet tracking system, the average website user will click about two to three times before becoming frustrated and going to another site or signing off completely. That doesn't give organizations much time to get the user engaged in the site - and the organization.

One important thing to consider here is that every day there are (or at least probably are) numerous members and prospective members going to websites and getting frustrated because they couldn't get the information they wanted. They may have been only a page or two away, but their frustration point (two or three clicks) had already been reached and they left the site.

Perhaps the worst part of this scenario is that organizations don't know who these people are. They can't be identified unless they are current members and have been asked to sign in to a members-only section of the site, so it is impossible to follow up with them.

Here's a suggestion: try to preempt this situation. Use the website's tracking information to find out which pages of the website get the most visitors, and which pages are the most popular, and reposition them. If the most popular pages are four or five clicks from the home page, move them closer. Make it as easy as possible for the highest number of visitors to get to the most useful part of the site.

Virtual members expect to be engaged with the organization in a quick, effortless manner. Don't leave them "*clicked off*" at the organization.

2) *Be sure to have an automated system of cross-selling set up to entice virtual members to be engaged in more than one aspect of your organization.* When members access the site and order a publication, have an automated acknowledgment that confirms their purchase and guides them to a part of the site that contains information on related topics (i.e. a video/CD library, an upcoming conference or educational offering, an online learning event, etc.).

3) *Each time a virtual member purchases something from the organization, whether it is a publication, a conference registration, access to an online educational program, etc., be sure to remind the member that as a virtual member a higher fee was paid than a regular member would have to pay.* Give the virtual member an incentive to become a regular member by offering to credit the extra money paid as a virtual member toward the first year dues as a regular member.

4) *At least twice a year take an online survey of virtual members.* Be sure the survey contains questions related to something of importance, rather than just questions about the organization's services. Try to let the virtual members know that their input is valued as much as the input of regular members. Be sure to acknowledge their input with an automated "Thanks for participating in our survey" message that is sent as soon as they complete the survey. Use their input to determine other ways they can participate.

5) *After taking a survey of virtual members, identify those who did not participate in the survey.* These may be potential drops in a few months when renewal notices are sent. Do some type of follow up with these nonparticipating virtual members.

6) *Offer virtual members ways to "attend" a couple of the organization's meetings online, to whet their*

appetite for future functions. Have real-time video or audio sessions on the website, so they can see and hear what they are missing.

7) *Put video clips on the web site after an educational program or conference.* Don't give virtual members all of the benefits of full membership but allow them to continually find value in some aspect of membership.

8) *Keep track of all participation by virtual members.* When they are sent their renewal notices (online, of course) remind them of how much money they spent participating in the organization last year and tell them how much *less* that was than a nonmember would have paid, but also how much *more* that was than a full member would have paid.

9) *Have a section of the website that is open only to full members.*

10) *Be patient.* Virtual members will probably be satisfied with their membership status at the beginning. Don't give up on trying to convert them to full members, but don't try so hard (and so frequently) that the organization is perceived as doing nothing else. Concentrate on getting them to see the value in virtual membership first. Just be glad they have been convinced to join in *any* category. It is a lot easier to get members to go from

one category to another than to go from being nonmembers to members.

Rule Number 13
Anchors Away

The leaders of an international manufacturers' association, headquartered in Washington, D.C., are worried about the organization's long-term viability. Like many other manufacturing industries, their industry has been going through several years of industry consolidation. This means that, for the most part, member companies are buying other member companies (the association represents 85% of the total industry). This, of course reduces the association's annual retention rate, since even organizations with the very best of retention programs find it hard to convince companies that are out of business to renew their membership. Needless to say, when the potential market for *new* members is already almost non-existent, keeping the current members is the only way to maintain a viable organization.

In this type of market, the organization has bent over backwards to accommodate its member companies. It has even established a flexible policy on dues collections, allowing companies which are struggling to stay in business to pay dues on a quarterly (rather than annual) basis.

Part of the organization's retention efforts center around enhancing the value of its meetings. The association concentrates on getting the very best industry experts to speak at the organization's meetings, giving members valuable information to help them better manage their businesses. One of the speakers that the organization sponsored presented a program on "lean manufacturing," a coordinated system of increasing productivity in the manufacturing field. During the presentation, the speaker noted that, in order to be really productive, companies had to infuse a new culture throughout their organizations, not just on the plant floor. This new culture had to include the participation of the organization's top management, he noted.

"In every organization," the speaker said, "there are three distinct groups of people. There are the leaders - the people who are supposed to be guiding the organization to fulfill its mission. These are the people who are supposed to be the visionaries, the people who get things done. Usually, this group represents about 10% of any organization."

"At the other end of the spectrum, every organization also has a group of about 10% of the people who are known as the anchors. These are the people who don't want to take chances, the people who say that 'We've always done things this way,' the people who don't want to change. They are usually the nay-sayers, who find fault rather than seeking solutions."

"The middle 80% of the people could go either way. If the leaders do a good job of leading, the followers will follow them. On the other hand, if the anchors have the strongest voice, the people in the middle will gravitate toward their point of view."

"Many organizations get into trouble," he continued, "because the leaders spend way too much time worrying about the anchors. They are afraid to do what they know is really the right thing because they are afraid of losing the support of the anchors, who can be very influential. The thing they fear most is that the anchors will actually quit - leave the organization. Most organizations don't want to risk losing *any* of their customers, members, supporters, or employees, so they tread carefully and try to avoid pushing the anchors to the point of quitting."

"What these leaders need to do," the speaker said, "is pretty simple: they need to lead. They need to take the action that is in the best interests of the organization, take the risk, and move ahead. What will happen is that the people in the middle will follow the leaders, **if** the leaders are decisive and forceful. This leaves the anchors with three choices: they can get with the program; they can get left behind; or, as the leaders fear, they can quit."

"Here is what the leaders should do: LET THEM GO! Let the anchors quit, walk off, resign, whatever. In today's marketplace, there is no time for organizations to get bogged down with negative thinking. If there are members, customers, or employees holding your organization back, LET THEM GO."

After the program, one of the leaders in the organization went up to the organization's staff director and said, "You know, that guy was talking about a manufacturing company but he could just as easily have been talking about our association. We spend too much time worrying that a couple of big members will drop out if we tackle any controversial issues. We need to let them go."

The leader was right.

It might seem like heresy to even consider the possibility that a nonprofit membership organization should let its disgruntled members quit. First of all, if the members are disgruntled, the organization should hear their viewpoints and see if there is some way to make these members happy. Second, even disgruntled members are better than no members at all – it's hard enough to get and keep members without chasing off the ones we already have.

It's time for things to change.

It is impossible for nonprofit organizations to be all things to all people, or all companies, or all institutions. Even organizations with well-defined, narrowly-focused membership markets find it impossible to please everyone. That's not the point. Perfection is not a realistic goal unless the organization has unlimited resources, and even then it's still probably not possible.

Membership organizations need to determine the point at which members have to make a fundamental decision to support the organization or (heaven forbid!) find another organization. In the beginning of this book, there was a discussion about valuing every member. That rule still applies – this is not a contradiction. Organizations should value every member, but they should also come to the realization that not everyone – or every company or institution - should *be* a member.

There are probably members in almost every organization who feel threatened by the changes that their organization has made. Some of these members are going to hold out until the bitter end. They want their organization to do things the way it has always done them, or else.

Or else what?

Or else they'll quit.

So, let them. It may be that in some organizations the cost and difficulty of servicing some members doesn't justify (even when the lifetime value of a member is considered) spending the time and money it will take to service them differently from all other members.

In other organizations, there are groups of members who are resistant to change. Why let young members in for less than the full membership fee, just because they can use computers effectively (i.e. virtual members), they wonder? Why create new membership categories - the old ones have been just fine for many, many years?

Should the views of these members be considered? Of course. But organizations aren't obligated to do what these members say, organizations are only obligated to give their views fair consideration. If the views of these members are considered, and the organization decides that it is in the interest of all members to go in a different direction, then the organization can't let threats of quitting stand in the organization's way.

Let them go.

It's not just older members, either. There is no age or generation or other demographic description that fits all anchors. Anchors can come in all ages, cultures, length of time as members, etc.

While challenges abound in the membership retention efforts that organizations face every day, so, too, do the opportunities. Organizations can't let the anchors become a barrier to member service, engagement, and retention. Cut the chain, and let the anchors go. Move on.

The only way to win today's Retention Wars is to use every resource available. Engaging members in a meaningful way - using every idea, method, gimmick, and technology available - is the cornerstone of successful membership retention programs. Once members become engaged, there is a chance they'll become involved. Once they become involved, there's an even better chance that they'll renew their membership.

Don't go into the Retention Wars unarmed. To better fight those battles, understand, and apply, the New Rules of Engagement.

Don't forget these other best sellers from the
Mark Levin Resource Library

Millennium Membership

Attitudes about membership-based organizations have changed forever. Only people who understand these changes --- and adapt to them --- will succeed in attracting and keeping members in the twenty-first century. But change is not your biggest challenge, it is the speed of change. In this insightful book, Mark Levin, CAE, CSP, explains not only how to adapt to the ever-changing marketplace but also how to make change work for you. The first six chapters of the book guide you through the steps you must take to succeed in recruiting and retaining members in the twenty-first century. The final chapter is packed with enough ideas to put you well on your way to membership success.

Forward by Harvey Mackay
Author of Swim With the Sharks Without Being Eaten Alive
"The power of association is a tremendous force in our personal and professional lives. . . Mark Levin shares his insight, experience, and talent to give his readers hundreds of suggestions on how to make the power of association work for them." --- **Harvey Mackay**

Membership Development: 101 Ways to Get and Keep Your Members

Tens of thousands of association, chamber of commerce and professional society leaders --- volunteers and staff members --- have benefited from Mark's unique, straight-forward approach to membership. Now this information is available in book, audio tape, or CD format. This is the information that is destined to become your best resource for helping your organization grow.

The Gift of Leadership

Every volunteer organization faces the same challenge --- how to attract and motivate that volunteer workforce. As the pressures of a 21st century society push in, the challenge becomes even greater. Now, for the first time, you can give your volunteer leaders both the inspiration and the information they need to be successful. Written by one of the world's most sought-after and respected speakers on volunteer organization management, this book is truly the "Gift" that your leaders deserve.

Order all these great books at *www.baileadership*